FULL CIRCLE

Looking at the world through my eyes

STEPHEN SUTTON

authorHOUSE®

AuthorHouse™ UK
1663 Liberty Drive
Bloomington, IN 47403 USA
www.authorhouse.co.uk
Phone: UK TFN: 0800 0148641 (Toll Free inside the UK)
*   UK Local: (02) 0369 56322 (+44 20 3695 6322 from outside the UK)*

Published by AuthorHouse   04/12/2022

ISBN: 978-1-4772-2747-3 (sc)
ISBN: 978-1-4772-2740-4 (e)

Print information available on the last page.

This book is printed on acid-free paper.

I wish to thank everyone involved in this book from those who inspire me to those who have allowed me the time to write it

CONTENTS

INTRODUCTION

*F*ull circle describes my life at present, looking back at my past and highlighting the more humorous activities of my life. My first book (Life in a jar—living with dyslexia) was about my disability and was based on factual evidence. My second book (Rise of the phoenix—a fathers story) was much more personal an discussed fatherhood. So full circle is lighter hearted and provides the reader with a look at my life from a different angle, based on my many accidents, and mishaps all over the world.

The object of this book is to never take life seriously, laugh at yourself and enjoy life as much as you can. The title describes many peoples experience in life, when have the habit of revisiting the past, maybe by chance or purposely return to the place they grew up. I often this happens when times are hard and they are seeking security, sometimes the past may hold the answers to why they are unhappy. Others seek the past to cling hold of precious memories that they had maybe in childhood, or as a teenager. Meeting old friends by joining 'friends reunited' online.

My past has been very colourful and a mixture of good and bad events like everybody else. Although I don't wish to discuss the details of my dilemmas I must say that I have suffered from a childhood of asthma, took an overdose at sixteen, been raped, came close to a breakdown at thirty and went through a bad separation at fifty. Despite all this and more, I managed to survive to tell the story. The secret of survival is to not allow past events to cloud your future, otherwise it will eat away at you and destroy the remainder of your life. Most people have good aspects of their life, things worth looking back on, in my case it was childhood hobbies, travelling, making new friends and bringing up my children. Today I am preparing and for filling my bucket list, doing all the things I want to do before I die, perhaps this sounds morbid but I just see it as a sense of completion, a way of saying look, I have done all I wanted to do.

This book outlines how I feel about this and other things, why I wind people up and torment them. The need to gain excitement by other peoples misfortunes or joke about certain peoples intelligence, but I am not cruel and only do things for fun. Its not my fault some people have no sense of humour or deserve being brought down due to their attitude. I always said that I would like to go on 'Big Brother' for that reason alone, because I think that was the most boring program ever broadcasted and the only way to motivate characters in BB is to wind them up. To be honest some people beg to be joked about by the way they act, like walking straight into a trap. Take for instance midlife crises what a subject to joke about, forty year old men and woman acting like teenagers, dressing like them and expecting other people to take them seriously. I don't think so, no, its more like they want to be laughed at.

By writing this book I hope to provide purpose in peoples lives by saying don't take life too seriously, make the most out of your life and enjoy yourself. Life is too short to dwell on past events or to gaze into space and look at the stars, thinking I wish I had done this or that. It is easier to go out and for fill your dreams, have the confidence to do what you really want to do. Only you can stop yourself doing things, you can only blame yourself if you don't do it, the opportunities are there, take them.

So why have a past at all, why do we remember our childhood or events from our past. Is it relevant to our present life, can we learn from the past in some way, or is it significant to future events. Why do people dwell on the past and find it difficult moving on?

Read on and try to understand what some people think about reliving or revisiting the past, why some people fail to move on and become so absorbed in the past that it prevents them from living a normal life. Past trauma's affect them so badly that they experience nightmares and panic attacks, some create phobias which lead to further complications. But is living or remembering the past so bad for all of us, even those who have not experienced problems, is it so harmful to relive any experiences from your past.

Full circle is designed to make you think about this and debate about the subject of reliving the past and the theories behind such controversial subjects as reincarnation. It is also designed to spark some thoughts about living a life that will be part of your past one day, and how to capture such moments and remember them for the rest of your life. This book demonstrates why we should chase our dreams; make good memories for ourselves by making plans for holidays and doing the things we truly want to do. Only by doing this we can reach full circle. I hope you enjoy reading this book even if you just laugh right through it. So keep on laughing and as Eric Idle of Monty Python fame would say 'always look on the bright side of life'.

CHILDHOOD

*C*hildhood is that strange time when you are guided by your parents, influenced by their life style and behaviour. We mimic them until we go to school and become acquainted with other children and their ways. We endeavour to seek attention to ourselves by behaving in certain ways, whether it is by behaving well or badly as long as it's some form of reaction.

What we fail to realise is that we are creating our past, although we may not remember any of it. The many Christmas's and other family events that are traditional and stand out in our lives, produce lasting memories for our future. Types of music that can trigger memories of past experiences both good and bad. This can also be so with smells, tastes and array of other things. But why do we have memories, what is the significance of having a past to remember?

We initially live with my grandparents who were my father's parents in Birmingham my parents had nowhere to live so we all lived there. I remember living there and some of my childhood years though it's only small memories of playing inside and out and eating jiffy jellies bought in glass containers. Though my memories are vague I know I was happy there and I especially loved my grandmother Sutton, she was so kind to me and so loving. I never wanted to leave there but my parents needed their own home and eventually when I was nearly five years old we moved to Lichfield. IT was then that I was to start school.

SCHOOL DAZE

I can only say that my early school years consisted of me being in trouble and bullied with no real reason, just that I was considered lazy, stupid and unwilling to learn. I was confused, frustrated and had no idea either that I had dyslexia or what the hell it was. It was not only an unknown word but a condition that never existed, times were hard and I had to cope with this unknown condition. Poor concentration and poor short term memory was the Bain of my life and god was I made to suffer for that. Given the ruler across the hand or slapped around the head for forgetting something or day dreaming. God knows what would have happened if I had committed a murder, maybe made to build a scaffold in the playground and hang for such a crime.

So pathetic, I must confess I did develop learned behaviour from other pupils so the odd slap was justified. Sometimes I was framed. My best mate Richard Howarth witnessed my punishments though he was never chastised from what I remember. Knocking down the mobile for remedial class was the best thing Chadsmead school ever did, I would have burnt it down myself had I had the chance.

MOVING UP

We faced the big school together stood in a large assembly hall mouths wide open as we tried to take in the sight. This was Netherstowe the 'big' school and what an under statement. Then to enter our first classroom with our form Mr Griffiths and given our first year time table, going to different classes for lessons was a novelty after being in remedial class in a hut away from the main school. We were no longer isolated and were part of the main school, this was frightening at first, but we soon adapted. I did have to attend remedial group for an hour or so each day, but the teacher there was confused as to the degree of help I required. I had formed my own strategies of coping with reading writing and spelling, I taught myself at home with English and American comics. I observed the bubbles with writing in that pointed to each character on a page and worked it all out, it wasn't hard, infact nothing visual was hard. Only the written word, damn English language is so bastardised its untrue, a combination of languages from all over Europe going back as far as the Saxons and maybe further.

So onward and upward as I leave remedial group more confused than when I went in. Oh I know they were trying to help but I could help myself always have done and always will. I continued to get into trouble for various things, but the rebel was out now and they may as well of hung me back in junior school. Well such is life not all was bad and I did have very happy times too.

Our memories store valuable information like a computer, things we need to know in our chosen careers and daily life, we memorise routines and store things from our past sometimes to reflect on or to learn from. Often something's like smells, pictures or music remind us of days gone by. Some things stay with us while other things fade away, depending on how much or how important the event meant to us. Some people try to block bad moments out but traumatic events bring them back.

Sometimes people seek happier moments when they are in despair, thinking of happier days by looking at photographs for comfort or playing memorable music. It's a sad fact that some people cant look back due to painful memories at home or school, it very much depends on the environment they lived in at the time. We tend to reach mid life or beyond and then look back, perhaps its then that we realise our own morbidity and think well not much more life to go so you go back and reflect on your life. Some go to extremes by returning to their roots, revisit their birth place or even go back to live there. This can be good if the place hasn't changed too much, but times change and places change. Don't be surprised if your old school is replaced by a mosque or that half the quaint shops have gone that what is known as progress. Or its about who cares about sentiment lets knock the place down and build a road there.

Childhood memories are often about family unity Christmas, Easter or holidays. It's a fact no matter how hard up your family are they will often make sure you have a good time, scrimp and scrape so that you are cared for properly and it's a joy to see children with happy faces. I speak of course by experience as my childhood was happy I played for hours with tiny plastic soldiers, painting them and listening to the latest music of the time on radio.

IN MY DAY

We lived in a flat at the time, right in the corner of a block of three story (Greencroft) flats in an 'L' shape with a big dirt area in the centre. It was a communal setting and most neighbours were friendly. Downstairs lived the Sutherlands who were probably the closest family to us young Jennifer was the same age as me. We were friends and often played together as kids, I particularly remember her toy post office. Another child friend was David Wilborn who always wanted to be a vicar, when I once ran away from home I hid behind his dustbin. In those days it was the sixties the fashion and music influenced us greatly the Beatles were big then and all sorts of material things came out like Beatle books, clothes even plastic wigs. I went into hospital to have my tonsils removed bled like I don't know what, spent time in the local (Victoria) hospital what a waste of time that was they have grown back now. Mr Worsey who own the local news agent in Lichfield came in regularly to deliver comics and papers.

We used to watch the television which was then in black and white and consisted of three channels, not many programs were interesting but we used to watch Dr Who which had just come out then, A lot of westerns that were popular at the time like Lone Ranger, Maverick etc and later when we moved to Bloomfield crescent we would watch the Munster's, Bewitched, Man from uncle and the Monkees. Gerry Anderson was also creating puppet shows like Thunderbirds, sting ray, and later Captain Scarlet.

We also watched family shows like Sunday night at the London palladium and an array of comedy shows like Tony

Hancock I would have sweets on Saturday and pudding on Sunday. Mother used to bake cakes and we had fruit salad for tea. Family times were good and my father made sure we were educated. He had an incredible mind and had good general knowledge; we used to play a game devised by Readers digest about guessing the meaning of unusual words. Family board games were another past time pursuit monopoly, scrabble or even card games. I also continued these with my children.

I may have had a rough time at school at times but I made the most out of play time chasing girls around the field and mobile hut, girls like Jean Barmer who I see today and remind her of such events. Although I spent most times with my new friend Richard who was introduced to me by my teacher at the time Mrs Coalman who said look after him. Richard Howarth and I remain friends to this day although he lives in Yorkshire and I live where ever. I say this because I am always on the move if I could drive perhaps I should live in a camper van.

I was a little rebel at times as a child and when I entered senior school I was like a cannon or a bottle of pop once roused I went off causing chaos. I went on the school roof after a ball, someone alerted me that teacher was coming so I threw the ball in, jumped in face down and slid across the desks onto the floor. I insulted the care taker ran away from him, while he was chasing me I dived through loads of coats in the cloak room and fractured my arm. I was on my way to school one day smoking at the outer gate, when I saw the head teacher at the inner gate He had seen me and it was a cainable offence at the time. I had a nose bleed and raced past him holding my nose shouting 'Cant stop, nose bleed'.

In science class I was running round and went crashing into the class skellington the teacher caught me and said "You innocent little blue eyes stand outside now!". I went out the class only to find the deputy headmaster outside I said just going to the toilet sir and walked off when I returned he was still there. He said go into class then and I replied I can't sir and explained why. He sent me straight to his office to be punished, more recently I have seen him on the quiz show 'Ask the family' with his family. But the worst bad deed I did was to play strip poker in class, five of us decided to play strip poker and I was unaware that they had been cheating. I had gone to the toilet dodged a teacher en route by climbing above the door and suspended from the window above clinging on for dear life. When I was absent they plan to set me up by cheating at strip poker. I was down to my under wear one of the girls had removed her shirt and as I took my trousers off put her shirt back on the teacher came in and I hid under the desk. In drama we all took it in turns hiding in a basket but when it was my turn someone sat on the basket, the teacher came in at me shouting "Let me out you daft twat" this resulted in another trip to the office.

HAVE AN ACCIDENT

I had accidents outside school too, I remember my friends and I throwing bricks and stones at a barn roof knocking the slates off, people used to pass and tell us off. When we went into the barn to collect our ammunition I continued to collect bricks while the others went out. Unfortunately they continued to throw their bricks and one bounced off a nearby wall and hit me just above my left eye. When I went out the main barn door on the other side they thought I was pretending to be hurt, but when they saw the blood streaming down my face they knew what had happened. Feared of the consequences they asked me to make up a story, so I said that a cart wheel fell off the wall and hit me on the head. Such an elaborate cover story and I thought people would believe me what a numpty.

I used to smoke as you have read before but I tried to conceal many things from my parents, so on one occasion I was walking home and spotted my parents coming I had a cigarette in my hand so I had to get rid of it quick. Panicking I put it in my pocket I thought I had put it out until it burnt a hole in my trouser pocket and burnt my leg.

Accidents were certainly my thing and the hospital might as well have saved me a bed because I was sure to be back there. I borrowed someone's chopper bike and was cycling around the area I went downhill speeded up just missed a police car and went up the ramp of a delivery van. On another occasion I went through a wooden fence but that was on my own bike. People would see me in bandages or with my head dressed and say 'have an accident and I would reply no thanks I've just had one'

I have always said if I had turrets as a child I would get caught out randomly swearing at someone in church or in a pub because I am so clumsy. Honestly I must have had a deaf and blind guardian angel because if I shouted god help me things got worse and boy did I suffer. The guardian angel missed everything as always maybe she was on vacation or sent to the wrong person, all I know is she wasn't with me.

POOR MEMORY

My dyslexia as a child affected my short term memory and concentration which was awful especially as I didn't know what was wrong with me at the time. My mother would send me to the local shops Gilliam's the newsagents, Mr Salt the butchers, Stanton's greengrocers or Charlie's corner shop. I would get similar items but never the right one, bacon was sausage, peas were beans and if I had a list I miss read it or gave it to them leaving it at one of the shops. One day I got it all wrong and ended up going back with it all.

I liked art class at school anything artistic often I used to pluck up the confidence to chat up girls in there and tended to work with them a lot, nothing changes. I was asked to model in my tennis outfit with a girl. I was so self conscious with all the girls watching me I fixed my eyes across the room until the girl bent over after losing the tennis ball. That was it my Henry stood to attention and I could only hope no one saw it, there was a few whispers and sniggers from the girls which indicated my worse fear they all knew. Henry had let me down and I wanted to get out quickly my thoughts were I wish they would either draw faster or the bell would go for home time. As the expression goes saved by the bell, then the teacher said you can finish off if you wish, my heart sank at this point.

I must say that I am not an aggressive person unless provoked and people have to push me that little bit further. I was in the dining hall when the prefects were serving dinner at our table giving themselves more than others and me a lowly first year having a farty mouthful so I kicked off and unlike Oliver in Oliver Twist I didn't ask for more I gave them more right in the face. They all saw it one crappy meal flying across the table and landing right at both prefects. Needless to say I was sent out for bad behaviour and after that we went for our own meals served by the kitchen staff. I was also stabbed in the hand in the dining hall so I went at the person with my knife and was sent out again never to return. It was junk goodies after that from the local shop.

NO HOPE

I had my appendix out at the age of fifteen what an ordeal that was I never do anything easy. I began having severe pains in the stomach and believe me it was agony not just for me but my long suffering parents who heard the groins and wining coming from the toilet, they had been watching some horror movie downstairs and thought one of the monsters had paid a visit. After hours of rolling round the floor and pacing up and down the kitchen I was sent by my doctor into hospital. On arrival I was nervous and eager to know what exactly was wrong with me; my doctor said he thought it was appendicitis. After careful examination ha-ha the doctors in the hospital decided because I developed a rash that it was German measles and sent me home. Once I got home everyone was surprised including my mother who had gone with me to the hospital. The next day I was getting twinging pains I was on my way to school and decided to visit my doctor when he saw me he was shocked and wanted to know why I wasn't in hospital having my appendix out. When I explained about what happened at the hospital he was furious and ordered an ambulance to pick me up from home immediately. This time my father escorted me to hospital in order to make sure I got seen and sorted out. In the ambulance I was accompanied by another passenger who was having a heart attack, I must say I felt well compared to him. This time I arrived at the hospital and was examined and confirmed as appendicitis and operated on that day.

I woke up to find I was on intravenous fluids (a drip up) and a drainage bag hanging from my right hand side with a tube coming from my wound site. The bag stunk and as I discovered later was draining poison from my body. My appendix was about to burst and had I gone to school it would have turned into peritonitis and I could have died. Pleasant thought dropping dead at school maybe in science or history class, I can imagine how that would have gone down, another pupil drops dead at school bored stiff. I went from being on a ward with geriatrics to a convalescent ward with the view of a nearby graveyard, not far to travel if you don't make it due to the operation or hospital food. I was in hospital for a while due to x-ray results that showed a shadow on my lungs. I felt reasonably well until a patient on the ward suddenly died and was shipped off the ward and possibly into the nearby graveyard. Perhaps they keep graves open and just have a laundry shoot through the window straight into the grave, save any fuss like putting the screens round while the porters cart him off.

The good hope hospital, my word no wonder they call it no hope. I was in bed one day when the patient next door asked for a commode, when they arrived with it the nurses forgot to put the bowl inside and the poor man dropped his load all over the floor. It was awful my parents were visiting and heard the commotion such a mess and smelly, all the ward was shocked.

My grandfather Sutton visited me there, I was so pleased to see him and my as father told me later he hated hospital so it was a special visit. I made friends with the some of the patients and helped the nurses with providing drinks for them, I used to visit people on the female ward talking to them and generally getting to know about them. I was walking like an old man at first bent over due to the operation I remember a soldier from the British army there who had also had his appendix out. I used to alert the nurses if their was a problem on the ward, one day the toilet alarms were going off I had trouble finding the nurses and eventually found them all in the nearby kitchen having a break. They didn't seem pleased that I had disturbed them and said they would go and see who was in the toilet shortly. Later the next day I had my drainage tube removed and boy that was agony I am sure the nurse must have been ex German SS or something she looked like a sumo wrestler and took pleasure in pulling the mile long plastic pipe out slowly. She told me to relax as she wrapped it round her wrist and pulled again. It felt like she was pulling all my insides out all I could think about was being anywhere but in her hands and when it finally came out I sighed with relief. I have been to hospital many times in my life but had to say this was the worst experience ever. Whenever I see sumo wrestlers or torture chambers I think of her.

LEAVING SCHOOL

When I finally left school I threw my books in the local reservoir called Stowe pool, the grand ceremony was a private occasion with no guests. According to my English and Library teacher Miss Caines I had a library book of theirs I think it was a book on Charles the first as this was my last History assignment. She said that I wouldn't be able to leave unless I gave it back but I never found it and left anyway. I confess I was awful at this time and finished school with English, History and Art qualifications. I did go on to college on a pre nursing course but hated Tamworth college and spent most of my time round Tamworth or Lichfield in and out of record shops and cafes. I felt education had let me down but that could have been the opposite as I could not be arsed to listen to anyone and wanted to doss around aimlessly. Such as my early life as a teenager but worse was yet to come as I entered my working life with the biggest chip on my shoulder and thinking I was a rebel with a cause.

TEENRAGER

*T*eenage years are probably the worst times of anyone's life, mainly because you have raging hormones, acne and at war with society or adults who just don't understand you. I think teenagers should grow up away from normal society in a commune or some institution like the army or boarding school. I say that but I would never have survived the army or boarding school, so my theory is blown straight away. I had good parents who tolerated me and I tolerate my children, so better to play down any tantrums and mood swings, especially with girls as it may well be premenstrual tension. The no go area where people have been murdered for just speaking to some women and the lash of some women's tongues have been known to take a man out at fifty yards.

Teenagers or teen ragers are often mad with the world because society dealt them a bad pack of cards; they go to school and either do well or struggle to make the grade. I used to say I didn't ask to be born, on reflection it was the most selfish statement ever said, but I was so angry with life back then. No one could convince me that life was good and worth living, I went drinking under sixteen, smoked and explored the aspects of sex. I associated with drug addicts but never took drugs; my philosophy was to always be in control of body and mind. Although if you asked me about that under the influence of alcohol I would probably give you an incoercible reply, and puke on your shoes.

I had a varied group of friends as a teenager I used to go out drinking and stay at someone's house rather than go home late or drunk. Sometimes I would wake up in a strange room and study posters on the wall, this was a good indication as to whose room I may be in. Big posters of busty actresses or singers usually meant it was a lad's room, though I have woke up with lesbians. Posters of male pop stars usually indicated I was in female company, but I usually found underwear around the room or tripped over items like a bra or bovver boots. Age didn't matter to me as long as I didn't find false teeth in a container near me, or odd glass eye, or even la screwed off leg.

One of my experiences as a teenager was what I describe as finding my way, by this I don't mean my sexuality or religious convictions. But seeing out my own identity or who am I, by this I explored the avenues of my mixed up mind. I tried out new experiences like fishing; this was a disaster as I can't keep quiet for long. I went with friends to a private fishing lake near a farm; we walked miles through boggy woods until he said "Here we are". He was referring to a clearing I stepped over a log and put the basket down. He they opened up folding chairs and began to prepare the rods and bate wriggly fresh maggots and other items which I couldn't even describe. We settled down in our seats and prepared our sandwiches for lunch, but all I could think about was those wriggly maggots. Suddenly cold bacon butties and spam became less tasty and I was feeling the contents of my breakfast having a return visit to my mouth. After sitting bored out my skull for an hour I was just smoking a cigarette when the rod began to bend and the line got tighter. Just at that moment I felt a bite on my behind, I dropped the cigarette in my hand as I yelled and lost the rod in the water. One of the lads commented "What's up you got a bite then". To which I replied "Too right I got a bite something bit my arse".

After another hour which felt like three days passed, we all decided to go home, but as we stared to move I tripped over the same log that we stepped over before and landed in mud. We had travelled there by bike, at least two of us did, and the other guy rode up on a mope head. As I was a little shaken by my fall he decided to pull my saddle as we went up a steep hill, the problem was he continued to hold on down the hill them let go. He said something but I didn't quite hear what he said, suddenly I realised what he said when I hit a sign post and skidded across the road stopping at a bank. He must have said turn right at this bend, but he had let go too late and consequently I was injured. The bike had shot into a hedge and was buried in it, one of the guys pulled it out and the other picked me up from the road. I was shaken, grazed my face, arms, hands and knees, so needless to say couldn't ride the bike, and told them I was going to get cleaned up at a near by pub.

You would have thought that experience would put me off fishing, however since that time I have been all night fishing in Fradley Staffordshire and sat with someone who was fishing in a pool in Lichfield, but I must admit it's not for me. I don't like peace and quiet or gazing at a rod, waiting for fish to bite or to get gnat bites while I am waiting.

So fishing was not for me therefore I had to find an alternative hobby, snooker was my next challenge, as I was invited to play snooker at a club in Birmingham. The place looked pretty rough and I was introduced to a black man called Clarence, he was big and as broad as he was long. Clarence introduced me to his friends all black and good snooker players, but some of the roughest men that I had ever met. I considered even if I could play I would lose or risk getting beat up or worse. As it happened they were the nicest people I had ever met and once we had finished playing we all went drinking together. One of our regular haunts was the holly bush that was bombed by the I.R.A in the seventies, as it happened I would have been there that night, but I was ill on that day and didn't go.

I did however go into another pub nick named the barn, where gangsters used to go and many other undesirables. I had a transvestite trying to touch me up, offered drugs, saw guns under tables on peoples laps and prostitutes offering trade. I saw the most attractive girl on the planet that night and couldn't help staring at her, my friend said look around but don't stare, but she was so amazing. After a while one of my friends noticed I had been staring at her and nudged me.
"Stop staring you will get yourself in trouble" he said nervously. I averted my eyes then went to the toilet, on my return my friend said
"You were followed in there by that girl's boyfriend"
"I never saw him" I replied

At that moment her boyfriend returned and a gang of police followed him, it was a police raid suddenly everyone scattered we went through a side door. We left for the bus station and heard no more about the event until the next week when we returned in there. Apparently someone was stabbed outside answering to my description, he was attacked by this girls boyfriend obviously he thought the poor chap was me and I had fortunately left through a different door. That night I was watching my back from the moment I heard that till I went to the bus stop, which was late and both my friends and I missed the bus and had to walk eighteen miles home. I set out at eleven pm and arrived home at four in the morning, maybe later. From Birmingham to Lichfield is quite a trek and walking under spaghetti junction was eyrie to say the least.

So that's my snooker experience, did it put me off, no I played when I worked at Pontin's and continue to play to this day. Some say it's a load of balls but I like it, I do find that I am better at Pool, but I try and I like to watch others play. My friend Mick Morris takes me to watch him play; he plays in a team and is really good. The other team players are very sociable and we often have a chat afterwards about the match. It's so different from the Birmingham club and the away matches take me all around the local areas around Cannock and that region.

As a teenager I must confess I was more than a little rebellious, I felt the world owed me something and I was determined to get it. The idea of working, going home to my family was a bit old fashioned and so I went in and out of jobs for fun. I was also anti establishment and definitely anti bosses. I wasn't prepared to be told what to do by anyone and no one had the right to bully me, this was out of the question and not happening. So each time a boss tried to tell me off it was farewell and up yours mate. I became as popular as an extremely bad STD and as for the law; I was always being pulled in especially when I had long hair and an air force great coat. One night I attended a friends Halloween party, Lesley asked me along as a friend as I had been seeing a lot of her. I got drunk stuck my head in a bowl of water to get a apple (well known party game) and some idiot threw flour over my shoulder, I found out who did it and waited till he was kissing a girl below me and from the balcony I launched a pumpkin. I then went for a walk to try to sober up and felt very sick. I reached a green by a pub and Hughie there, suddenly I heard sirens and looked in front of me, and two police officers were coming towards me. God I must of killed the git with that pumpkin I thought and tried legging it, however no sooner had I turned when two other policemen grabbed me and pinned me to the ground. I wonder how many years you get for a pumpkin murder. These were my last thoughts as I struggled to move. Where have you just come from they asked me, well I was never going to get away with this one so I said a party. "Yeah" said one of them. You've been doing a bit of cat burglary one said; well I gave a sigh of relief and said what in a suit. He then turned me round and looked at me I know you he said. He did indeed he worked with my brother, at that he offered me a lift home; this must have been the earliest I had ever got home from a party.

I ran away to London got into trouble and came running back with my head in a symbolic sling, I had attempted suicide over a girl and lost my first job in a printing firm ironically I was printing hospital forms in a firm at a village called Alrewas. My language was colourful and choice of women bordered on weird so perhaps the combination of suicidal tendencies and being accused of being a drug addict turned my head. I won't discuss my London experience as a sixteen year old but suffice to say I have never forgotten it and still get nightmares to this day. it was quite an ordeal that has scarred me for life mentally.

But this book is supposed to be up lifting so may I say that my teens were definitely sex, not drugs and definitely rock and roll. I would stay out at night at friend's homes, get involved with women and enjoy my drunken teen years jumping from job to job but never sticking to one profession. I never took crap from anyone if someone pissed me off I would move on and try somewhere else.

I have worked in hotels, on farms, in factories and many other settings. I have had some brilliant experiences over the years and seen so many things which have taught me about people and their lives.

I worked on a pig farm mucking them out and was once chased by a boar around a pen, the boar rammed a gate, the gate hit me and he escaped. I used to consider pigs cute until I worked there. I also worked on a chicken farm plucking them yes I said plucking them, removing their feathers I had to chase a few too, catch them and take them to the shed for slaughter. I had to run catch their feet and bring them in but on occasions I fell over and was covered in chicken diddy. It was fun working with the women there though such characters and I did fancy one of them called Mary, she had dark hair, slim figure and rosy cheeks reminded me of snow white.

My factory experiences were something else one place was owned by a Hungarian who had his wife working there and would argue in Hungarian. His wife was nice but he was like a German Gestapo general fat old, fat and ugly as sin. He hardly spoke to me but told others to address me if I did something wrong which was often. I finally had enough when he was shouting his mouth off and I walked out and went to my favourite café.

My hotel experiences were short lived I was at the Belfry staying at the chateau which was a building near the main building where staff stayed. It was fun there I worked nights with other porters and did I see some sights. I was once called to a woman's room because of a ticking radiator when I arrived in the room she was wearing a see through night dress that was revealing more than expected. She was obviously after more than a spanner for the radiator. Well I suppose one of the perks of the job and it ticked until she checked out after a fortnight.

A woman got drunk at the same hotel and went into the men's toilet trying to use the urinal to pee on took me ages to sort her out, she was stuck on it and needed a lift off. Then a man was streaking around the hotel, he had lost his room, he couldn't remember where his room was and was drunk. One of the other porters helped him. On another occasion a drunk ran up the corridor to the main entrance and went literally straight through a window without hurting himself.

I saw quite a few celebrities at that hotel and a fair few snobs but hey everybody gets them and it's a free country so they say. Again I found it difficult taking orders and dealing with idiotic managers so I made comment and went my merry way to pastures new. The manager's name was Mr Cant but that's not what I called him as I made my final remarks known to him.

One funny event happened at the château my friends there had a party one of them was an ex nun presently a room maid the biggest sinner ever. We decided to play a prank on one of the kitchen staff and as he was drunk and unconscious put his bed on the balcony strip him naked and put him on top of the bed. We locked the door preventing him from getting back in then waited till morning. The next morning it was busy with all the traffic coming up the drive towards the hotel and he suddenly got up stretched and yawned then realise he was outside on the balcony and gasped 'What the hell's going on'

I was sent to a place that deals with people who have trouble getting or staying in a job called a re-establishment centre, probably another word for an open prison except you could leave if you get a job. This was in Henley in Harden near Stratford upon Avon, set back away from the main road a few roads in. It was a case of living in a room with a sliding door, the room consisted of a bed wardrobe and set of drawers at the end of the corridor was a toilet and door which was locked at 10.00 curfews. The guards or whatever they were called told us when to go to bed locked up and patrolled but it wasn't a prison. We got up in the morning to the sound of a bell and shouting and we had a shower and breakfast before we started work. The labour was hard and the breaks brief, I did gardening and was often caught smoking sat on the grass between hard labour so eventually I was sent inside to clean rooms. In the evening I used to draw and occupy my time chatting to the inmate's even one of the men said he had been in prison and treated better. I kicked of one day because I was given a salad with a green caterpillar in it, I don't do walking food and ok I was being punished for being a job dodger but I don't expect live grub. I eventually found a job and got out of there after all it had all manner of perverts and weirdo's there even one of the officers said I shouldn't have been there.

I even got sent to a rehabilitation centre in Coventry yes I was literally sent to Coventry. It was better than the re establishment centre but still faced with nutters and at least it was mixed sex so I went out with a nice girl. Got into a few fights in Coventry, in pubs and clubs with gangs and such. I had to kick a knife out of one mans hand and got thumped by a boxer on another occasion. All the fun of teenage years and all part of growing up but someday I would have to settle down and be mature, maybe get married and have children. I had always wanted children from the time I started baby sitting for friends I nearly got involved with one woman ten years my senior through baby sitting. I really liked her and she knew it she once left the bathroom door open knowing I would go in to use the toilet. She stood naked in the bathroom as I entered I stood surprised me a seventeen year old with someone in her mid twenties with the body of venues, my god. The imagination works overtime doesn't it; you get no more information this isn't fifty shades of grey you know.

The least said about my sex life the better Just because I have been known to frequent Victoria secrets and lived to tell the tale. And have known some of the kinkiest women around who have had more power tools than black and

Decker. I may have been rebellious but I knew when to behave at times and although immature I was sensible when it came to drugs. I had friends who took them and spent time in drug dens but never took them because I like to be in control of my body and mind. Yes teen years were pretty turbulent as were my relationships weird psychotic girls beautiful but dangerous I had to change for the better and turn my life around but how could I do this?

REACHING MATURITY

I found my teenage year's very trouble some as people around me would witness by sharing my frustration or rage. I was a true teenrager had the devil on my back and hated the world. But one day as I was sat watching mind numbing television a knock came at the door, I dragged my lazy body to the door and two ladies stood with bibles in their hand asking me if I wanted to live forever. What in this crappy world are you kidding I told them. I had been studying all sorts of religion from the conventional Christianity to less known beliefs like Rastafarian or Buddhism. I suppose you could call it searching for god, or a meaning to life. Anyway these were Jehovah's Witnesses telling me about living in a paradise earth, in peace and safety. Well I needed a change of life style desperately and these people seemed to have the answer at the time. So I was hooked, and spent a few years cleaning up my act, modifying my behaviour. Stopped smoking, drinking and swearing for a while.

I was a different person and was happy in my delusion that all was fine and I was protected in my JAR. This was shattered when some people's imperfections came out, they were quite hostile and were definitely not showing Christian feelings but like someone possessed Linda Blaire springs to mind in the movie Exorcist. So my experience at that time was mixed, although I was a different person I found it difficult living with hypocrites. I discovered a lot as a bible student and some was to my advantage, I find it difficult believing in a god who allows suffering to take place although this was explained to me in detail, my heart still says "why".

With my new found knowledge I settled into work in a care home, and remained there for thirteen years experiencing a different life style again. I was faced with cleaning bums for a living, very abstract and definitely alien to me at the time. I had only cared for myself and my own needs, keeping myself clean and tidy but never anyone else. I had to get used to working with women in a female oriented environment, it was a joy and now I would never work with men again. Yes there is bitchiness and back biting at times, but women poses a strange sense of humour that once you get to know the formula it really is funny.

It was at this time that I discovered I was dyslexic and began to understand why I struggled at school. I discovered the dysphasic side too as I was very clumsy. One day the gardener was off sick and the carers had to do gardening. We all took it in turns, weeding, planting and my dread mowing the lawn. I was asked to mow the lawn, but my last experience with a lawn mower I electrocuted myself. This time I started it up and it raced off pulling me across the lawn and I was dragged across lawn and under a hedge, fortunately the path stopped the mower taking me any further.

Another disaster was when I was given a tray full of breakfasts and I attempted to deliver them to residents in their rooms. The theory was good but the reality was something else as I headed down a flight of stairs and my shoe split, I went flying downstairs and all the dishes on the tray flew in all directions. The domestic who was cleaning at the bottom of the stairs reacted by saying
"What a bleeding mess".

I have been trapped in a lift there, slipped on the floor countless times and had more accidents than I can remember. The Matron used to call me Britain's last hope especially after I knocked her over in a corridor. I was showing a future resident round she was in a wheelchair so I wheeled her down the hall I was looking straight ahead, the Matron suddenly came out of the dining room and went into me flying right over the wheelchair. I was talking to the lady saying "This is the hall and bump this is the Matron".
Matron got onto her feet and shouted "You have ruined my new tights"
Changing course for me was not only calming down from a wild teenager, but getting used to being dyspraxic and dyslexia. I was now writing reports and had to spell awkward words like diarrhoea, I fast discovered I was not allowed to write slang words like shit. Although I was used to painting them on street walls and vocalising such things in public. To say faecally incontinent rather than he or she has just crapped themselves was alien to me, almost like learning a new language.

My biggest fear apart from the matron of course was false teeth, swilling peoples teeth was a horrible task. Just as emptying commodes and cleaning dead bodies. I remember

someone collapsing on the toilet both the other carer and myself was speechless; we carried her body across the corridor to her bedroom. She remained limp but defecated on the floor; we dodged the trail of faeces and put her on the bed. She suddenly popped up and said "I've shit".
We both thought she was dead and didn't want to alarm each other, but she was clearly not.

I also became known as a thespian often displaying a theatrical nature. I dressed up on many occasions such as Christmas, Easter, and Halloween and whenever it was called for. Open days, Strawberry fayres and Bower day were often an excuse to dress up. A theme was chosen like the Wild West open day or medieval day and we all dressed up, it was so much fun and we usually raised quite a bit of money. The Lichfield Bower at that time was a big day for Lichfield, that involved a fair, lots of stalls and people visiting from areas around Lichfield as far as Birmingham (despite what some people think Lichfield is not part of Birmingham) But the most spectacular part of the bower day festival is the parade, a series of floats drive along the streets decorated in a particular theme. All the floats are judged to see which is the most colourful, best designed etc in order to win a cup. First and second place get a cup and cheque for their efforts.
We come first place three times and second once, but we put so much time and effort into making our float look good. One year however we had dodgy breaks and despite winning we were thrown about the float for fun. We had chosen Dr Johnson's birthday as a theme guess who I was? Yes Dr Johnson but I was skinny at the time, he was fat, and so I padded myself up for the event. This meant every

time I stumbled I never hurt myself I hit the back ground scenery and people fell into me but I was fine.

I have dressed up as Dracula on a night out, dressed as Quasimodo giving others the hump, I have been Robin Hood at the medieval fayre, a medicine man in a wild west open day and much more. My many roles and performances will be remembered like Henry V111, Santa and others. But my best experience was as a 17th century puritan at a sealed knot event, I attended at the Kings head Lichfield. I had shared quality time with them re enacting a trial at the town hall and drinking with them at the kings head where they usually had meetings. I left there and headed past an old church called St Chad's I decided to walk through the graveyard and came out over a stone wall, a couple were sat on the wall saw my ghostly shape and the boy ran leaving the girl behind. I carried on and arrived at my house; I went in for the dog and walked him over a bridge. A car suddenly pulled up and the driver wound down his window. He looked at me then the dog and said "Either I am pissed or you're a ghost".
I replied "I am a ghost".

I also got involved in a lot of charity work writing songs for them and spending time on television and radio, I also wrote songs about my life and other people's experiences. 'I can't understand you' was one such song written about a friend separating from his girl friend. Or 'Ambitious dreamer' which is about my life as a teenager, and my desire to do something with my life. And in a way I have achieve so much in writing books, going to university and travelling around the world. I may not have been so successful in marriage but that's life you can't be good at everything, at least I was ok as a father.

Speaking of travel I started to show an interest in travel years ago and its now in my blood, I am hooked I love it and so do my children. It is thought to broaden your mind. Seeing cultures and a varied style of life, different to your own, travelling across vast states, provinces and continents. Visiting the wild life and that's just in the main cities, as people run riot across the busy streets.

Religion can be a comfort, a way of straightening your life out and a safe zone if you're feeling vulnerable. The teachings of the bible can be adapted to society, but some aspects conflict with today's ideas of look out for yourself because no one else will. The suggestions of turning the other cheek or being humble shows a weakness in principle, to allow people to treat you badly and just take it on the chin. And within religions there is always an eccentric who thinks they are some sort of saint, disciple or prophet, which is why people tend to turn away from religion not towards it. The ones who consider that they are more Christian than others and criticize your Christian standards.

Religion in no matter what form is based on the belief of a god, a higher power of intelligence who is worshiped by imperfect human beings who seek guidance in times of trouble. This is the basic fundamental reason why we seek god, we are lost souls who need to believe in something, our thoughts and sometime heart yearns for an existence of a maker. History shows how people need guidance to exist in an imperfect world. But some believe in evolution suggesting than man came about by chance and not by a super human design, they call it the big bang theory. The evolution process is very evident when you see some people who resemble apes or fish and could very easy come from swamps but is it feasible and could we have appeared by chance. Who knows perhaps the answer is completely different and sooner or later another theory will emerge involving parallel existences with people of like kind co existing presenting ideas that have to date not been thought about.

Let's say another race of beings totally different from ourselves created us as an experiment and put us on this earth. The earth at this stage was cooling down and in its raw state, the dinosaurs were used to shape the earth and these aliens considered it good for habitation but not by them. So they formed humans creating them in a laboratory from cells and ensured they could reproduce at this point they're own planet exploded and they died leaving the human beings to fend for themselves. At the same time they instilled into the initial man an existence of a higher power or being thus the need to worship or seek a god.

I must say I keep an open mind regarding religion and the existence of god but I am concerned about the arrogance of some people who think what they believe in is right and others are wrong. I admit I was helped by religion, my life stabilised but who's to say if I had married I might have done so anyway. I went through a stable but strange time with religion and reserve the right to stand say I really don't know if I did the right thing at the time, I know that things happen for a reason but is that a cliché and something that holds no weight. Who knows we all abide the law and the law suggests not killing etc but someone once said as long as you follow the Ten Commandments you can't go wrong, well that's most of us screwed isn't it. Also look at many religions and tell me which ones have been at war or fighting catholic against catholic for example, what an example they are setting. The whole idea of religion should be considered and god knows what the answer to that will be.

My experience with the Jehovah's witnesses was good and bad, I had become one of them, the ones people called 'Jobos' or the 'god squad' many more names came forward as I joined the ministry (door to door work) At first it was scary knocking on doors and discussing the bible, but I soon settled down and spoke to some very nice people. Of course not all people greeted me with open arms, I had the usual verbal abuse and the door slammed in my face. The look of disgust and what stone have you crawled out of, but this did not deter me as I went on my quest to find fellow Christians. I spread the message and spent many hours sharing recently accumulated knowledge all seemed to be going well for a while.

My life was changing and the animal inside was becoming tamed, all my previous rebellious years seemed so distant although only a year before I was in that hotel giving the staff I hated so much grief and sorting peoples problems out like our lady with the ticking radiator. Then one day as I was in the ministry I was verbally insulted by one of the women with me who we referred as a sister (the men were brothers, Christian family thing) She was quite offensive and people knew it and just said that's her, its her imperfections. I considered her a horrid bitch who thought she could treat everyone like dirt. This continued for some time until finally she changed congregations and gave them grief instead.

Unfortunately she was not the only person who was a bad apple others had been involved in petty theft and upset neighbours by their bad language and abuse. Clearly the cracks were appearing in this perfect environment and decay set in. Solidarity amongst the ranks out of Christian unity was experiencing a divide and I was becoming disillusioned by the whole idea of one big Christian family who stuck together and protected their own kind. Also I had come across much more hostile householders on the ministry and some a little weird. One woman was a true religious fanatic who took me back to my early teens and experience when my friends and I were taken to a Pentecostal church, we didn't know where we were going then and had such a shock. We thought we were going to some youth club until everyone kept shouting Hallelujah! Well we kept jumping wondering what was going on, couldn't wait to leave there. This woman at the door was clearly that type a blonde version of Kate Bush shouting in a singing voice 'Unbelievable' and waving her arms about. Another women we met as we travelled in twos was a Satanist, she was chanting and enticing us into her home having objects and symbols of Satan. She much reminded me of past girl friends who had all kinds of strange ideas and well enough said.

I did make a lot of friends at this time but I must confess I felt suffocated by the experience after all how can you be perfect in an imperfect world. I admire those who can be like that, trying to live outside the corrupt world and live Christian lives but like communism its alright in theory but in reality its hard to live up to ideals and principles. Children who grow up in the faith struggle to fight for their principles at school and in adult life face the same challenge at work as they are ridiculed for what they believe in. I missed too many things in the world and felt trapped in what I would say was a false world of idealistic principles and yearned for adventure. I do value this experience and will not forget the kindness that some had shown me, also it did straighten my life out.

WORLD TRAVEL

*W*hen I was once approached at work by a colleague slightly older than myself, who took pleasure in telling me about her adventures abroad. I was slightly envious and although a little apprehensive about taking on such a trip. It was expensive for one thing and saving money was not something I did well. Liz had travelled on the orient express across Europe to Italy, the Orient express was a luxury train that in the eighties not well known to the poorer classes. So I kept declining and continued frequenting bars and clubs for my entertainment.

However after a few years I reconsidered and began organising my first trip abroad, I book a coach trip across Europe destination Italy.

It was the cheapest way to travel and I was guaranteed to see the sights this way, starting from Holland through Germany and Austria.

What I didn't was travelling across by coach was hazardous to ones health; I don't particularly mean the road when I say this. After all my first trip was definitely a suicidal one full of danger and intrepudation, because travelling with others required putting up with so many personalities and some people were definitely weird. They say travel broadens the mind and I would agree with that after my many experiences, this trip in 1983 was no exception. My objective was to reach Italy in one piece and not be subject to being mentally battered by the sound of Max Bygraves greatest hits pounding out of the speakers and a group of old age pensioners as backing vocals singing out of tune.

Then the coach driver announcing on the microphone that he was about to travel through rough roads with air pin bends across the Austrian mountains and playing the hymn 'abide with me'. I noticed the odd few people praying and some writing wills. It is possible to make friends with some of the people and I was friendly with a Yorkshire man and his son, the young lad had learning disabilities and was a happy young chap. Another family was a Lady who reminded me of Hilda Baker with both looks and mannerisms, she had brought along her son, or did he bring her along?

Leaving England for the first time seemed strange as the ferry travelled over the English Channel to the Hook of Holland. I was amazed at all the miles of flat country as we journeyed through Holland and entered Germany on the autobahn, then arrived at the picturesque Rhine valley. I was eager to have my photograph taken with the River Rhine in the background, so I immediately passed my camera to the Yorkshire chappy called Bill. I leaned on a pole and tried to look natural, suddenly the pole began to rise and I was soon in mid air yelling get me down. I later discovered it was a barrier for a level crossing between the Rhine and a railway track.

Hospitality was good in Germany, I only had one bad encounter which was with a big German waitress, and she reminded me of Basil Fawlty a character created by John Cleese. Very rude and abrupt demanding we sat down and moving us from table to table, poor Hilda Baker was dizzy by the time she finished. I visualised her in a Nazi uniform wearing a monocle and waving a stick at us, silence you svines and tell me what you want. The food was really good but Mrs Fawlty was inclined to give you indigestion, every time she entered the room someone choked.

Once we left Germany we heading for the mountains which I described earlier with the air pin bends across the Austrian landscape famous for the film the Sound of music picture Julie Andrews running down a mountain singing the hills are alive and then replacing Julie for a under study Hilda Baker. No I am not mad I announced when I laugh out loud at my bizarre imagination. But come on the sight of a little plump dark haired 65 year old woman bouncing down a hill, singing out of tune must affect your chuckle box.

When we were at the hotel at Landeck in Austria our second place of rest after the Boppard in Germany. I was disturbed in my room by knocking at the door; it was Hilda's son, come quick he said. To which I replied even I can't perform miracles. I followed him to his mother's room expecting a corps or a waiter hanging from their ceiling after a long conversation with Hilda about her cat. Instead there was Hilda bent over the bed with loads of coins on the mattress, she seemed to be sorting them out. Can I help you I asked her, and by the way her name coincidentally was Hilda, she immediately responded "Ohhh Steve thank god", I must confess I have never had such an effect on a woman like that. I am trying to sort my coins out and can't figure out which coin belongs to which country. I might add at this period of time the euro had not reared its ugly head and so each country had its own currency that we had to change each time we entered a new country from Holland to Germany to Austia and Italy. No wonder the poor old dear was confused. She continued I have all countries even Spanish potatoes, she meant Pesos, but mind was driven to overdrive once more and I visualised her using potatoes in exchange for other goods like postcards, Hilda with her bag of spuds in a tourist shop saying how many potatoes for each card. However as it happens we were not even going to Spain so why she needed Spanish currency was beyond me.

Hilda was also inclined to speak loud which did annoy the local people somewhat, a gang of Austrians became hostile at the sound of her voice in a bar. She was oblivious to this as a few of us challenged these men saying she has the right to speak and to leave her alone. Although sometimes we were deafened by her voice at times. We also had the opportunity to venture up a mountain in a cable car this was quite exciting as I had never done this before. Also it was the same cable car used in the film 'Where eagles dare' starring Clint Eastwood or as Hilda would say Waywood. As I entered the car before me was a wheel barrow full of cement I squeezed in and to my horror was joined by two of the largest women I have ever met. Big sweaty bodies pushing against mine, not my idea of a Clint Waywood movie, more like final destination. Needless to say the entire experience was bad, and I was thin then and coming out my body had become paper thin, all my organs crushed and starved of oxygen. When I arrived at the café at the top of the mountain I was hungry and thirsty. For the first time I came face to face with the language barrier when I looked at the menu. All in

Austrian perhaps those woman could help I thought to myself, but then I thought they might make me pick up the tab. They looked as if they could consume the entire menu between them, and I get the bill. I decided to take a chance and go for a safe bet and order a burger. Big mistake the burger ended up to be snaps a farty glass with a very strong liquor appeared on the table, I thought they were being hospitable and drank it. Well my mouth was on fire; I was as much out of breath as when I was in the cable of horrors, belting out flames like a dragon. I asked where my burger had got to and they replied I had had it, god talk about fast food it was so fast I didn't see it. Of course eventually I realised what had happened swept my dignity off the floor and left for the cable car. With the dread of entering the cable car, to my relief I travelled alone minus the wheel barrow.

Eventually we arrived in Italy at the picturesque Lake Garda, where romantic people often go for their honeymoon. The lake is surrounded by fine buildings tiled roves and a castle in Seralamone, Lemone has many lemon trees and we stopped at a hotel in Gardone. I spent a about ten days here touring and taking in the scenery including Venice known for its canals and gondolas and Verona which was famous for Shakespear's inspiration of Romeo and Juliet, featuring the famous balcony where Juliet called out to Romeo. But Lake Garda will remain memorable for the electric storms that lit up the entire lake. All the tourists ran for cover while Italians just walked along the side of the lake unaffected by the thunder and lightening. Another event there was when I jumped on the roof to rescue a cat, and the cat leapt off leaving me stranded. Or when I drank too much and fell out of bed bruising my ass. Or seeing a fish flying in the air only to find out it belonged to a fisherman who was throwing them over a wall.

I enjoyed my holiday so much I went to France and Spain at the end of the same year, destination Calella near Barcelona. This time I befriended an English lorry driver who had a few tales to tell of his many driving jobs. One involved taking a giraffe from one place to another; he had to use a rope around the giraffe's neck in order to make the animal duck as he entered low bridges. But we experienced a really odd couple on this trip they were both alone initially but got together and unwillingly began to entertain the rest of us. She was talking about her cat swallowing poly filler and we imagined the cat suddenly going stiff like a Tom and Gerry cartoon. Some people just can't help entertaining others by either what they say or by their actions. One of the biggest problems however was Spanish tummy, a nasty affliction of the bowel. The Spanish knew exactly how to deal with this at least the hotel staff did, due to so many cases each season. The hotel desk and lobby area had a set of spiral stairs running down into a toilet area, the object was when they saw someone walk down nothing happened, but when someone ran down staff armed with air fresheners suddenly ran to the stairs and all sprayed the area. Great clouds of mist suddenly polluted the ozone, and so if you didn't fall victim to the ghastly smells you choked on the fumes.

I laughed as people fell prey to the dreaded Spanish tummy each day, until on the last day it was my turn breaking wind was so fearsome due to a thing called follow through. I must have had so many accidents, running down the spiral stairs only to find the toilets full. Then the lift was always occupied so I ran to the floor that I was on, it would be the fourth floor and struggling with my key in desperation in case I didn't make it.

I left Spain having been to a knights pageant and watching jousting tournaments. We journeyed to France and arrived in Paris seeing the many sights including the Eiffel tower where I nearly got arrested walking on the grass being chased by the French police.

Holiday number three was not as adventurous although I did go on yet another coach trip, as if I hadn't been punished enough. This time the passengers really excelled themselves at annoying me, what a mixed bag of complete arseholes. One delightful lady was sat right behind me and every time she decided to get up she pulled my seat back.

On one occasion she had a cup of water in her hand and spilled the contents over my shoulder, no apology perhaps she was upset because she missed my head. She was a big noise in her local council and made sure everybody new it, by announcing the fact and displaying her authority. We were heading again through Europe to Florence in Italy, when we arrived she complained all the time about the amount of people who couldn't speak English. Even in the most remote parts of Italy. I said would you expect people in England to speak Italian, trying to reason with her by using human logic this fell on deaf ears of course. She was diabetic and wanted every packet of goods translating into English, and would fill her bags full of food from each restaurant. She was a mobile grocery store. She was so popular everyone clambered for a seat to be next to her, I had a choice of listening to her or Max Bygraves, yes the choice of music resorted with the famous Max and his old bull and bush. I at this time had contemplated the many ways to commit suicide from shooting, stabbing or lying in the aisle of the coach and being trampled down by the elderly.

Having survived the 1984 coach journey I dared to venture across Europe once more, 1n 1985 I went again to Italy this time to Rimini on the east coast of Italy covering Riccione and an independent state in Italy called San Marino. However this time I was fortunate enough to meet younger people and went to pubs and clubs in style. The only thing that went wrong this time was I got bad sun burn and my legs swelled like inflatable balloons. I was climbing mountains like the Michelin man in so much agony, each foot step felt like a moon walk.

In 1986 I had the opportunity to go to the U.S.A, the plan was to get a ticket on the famous greyhound buses and randomly stop at places all around America. I succeeded in visiting such places as New York, Washington, Richmond, Orlando, New Orleans, Dallas, Houston, Los Angeles and Nashville. As well as places in between the whole experience was fantastic and one of my best holidays ever. Needless to say it was not without the odd hiccup I literally bumped into a man in a tuxedo and almost knocked him down some steps in Beverly Hills. The man was heading towards a hotel for a wedding reception; I later discovered this man was non other than Johnny Carson the famous American chat show host. I found out this days later when I was

watching television in Nashville, I was flicking through
their many TV channels and there he was hosting his show
'The Johnny Carson show.

I met many strange people on my travels someone once
claimed to know Princess Margaret and others just knew
aliens and smoked cannabis with the Beatles or Rolling
stones. The word bull shit springs to mind of course, I think
they see the English as gullible they always think everyone
in England comes from Liverpool and know the Beatles or
the Queen.

I met Gloria in Richmond in a black community; she
reminded me of Diana Ross and was a wonderful lady who I
could have spent the rest of my life with. However I wanted
to see so much of America and always thought that I would
return to her. Despite this Gloria had the pleasure of my
company or rather I had the pleasure of hers. She showed
me around her home and when we entered the kitchen
she phoned her friends and family and told them that a
white man was staying who had travelled from England.
Then she call me and said could they all come round to
visit me here, I agreed and suddenly a kitchen full of people
came in to view the white man from England. Before long
we were conversing about America and England and the
environment was filled with smoke not from ordinary
cigarettes but cannabis I got so high I swear I rose up to
the ceiling, my imagination was working on overdrive and I
thought while I was up their I could change the light bulb.
We had a great time and a double for Huggy bear from the
hit series 'Starsky and Hutch' kept me entertained. When
the time came to leave I wouldn't say Gloria didn't want me
to leave, but she may as well greased the door knob, hit my
feet with a sledge hammer or nailed me to the front door. I

did stay longer and in view of our relationship could have stopped, but I had to move on in order to visit the rest of America, at least some of it.

My most memorable moment with Gloria apart from our trip to Richmond and Washington was when I was trying to cool down in bed. She went to fetch me a jug of grape juice; I was lying in bed trying to find the switch to the fan. She came back in and crawled across my body wearing skimpy silky night wear, just above my head was a cord she pulled it and the large fan above my head connected to the light spun round. It was noisy and I felt if it came down spinning it may cut a few bits off, so needless to say I didn't sleep too well. At least that's y excuse and all I would tell you. Sufficient to say I have never experienced anything quite like this one and I will never forget Gloria. I continued to Florida, New Orleans where I met Anja a life long friend, I continued to Texas, Arizona and California. Where I literally bumped into Johnny Carson the famous American chat show host and visited the homes of the rich in Beverly hills (from the road and not actually in their homes of course). From there I travelled to Nashville.

When I got to Nashville I ventured out to many places alone, one of the experiences was walking over a very high bridge to the famous museums etc, I nearly died going over it I just looked ahead and tried to avoid looking down. I decided to avoid the bridge going back and got lost; I did however find a dirt track and a rail way line. I thought it was strange as there was a platform decorated with red, blue and white flags and banners. Suddenly many cars arrived and soon I was surrounded by a crowd, god what a reception they must know I am from England. I discovered after questioning a few people that it was something to do with the governor's home coming, a band appeared and the crowd applauded.

My return flight from America was harrowing I had watched a man discussing the fluctuating wing and as he had never flown before thought the wing was going to drop off. But that's not what bothered me, as I was adjusting my arm rest it came loose in my hand and I had contracted a sore throat so was unable to communicate effectively. The stewardess eventually caught on and moved me to another seat; I was comfortable until I went to move my seat back to rest. The seat shot back and I ended up with my head between women's legs behind me, I was unable to speak and groined. She yelled out and the same stewardess came to me, with a face of disgust, she took me back to my original seat and seemed to be watching me for the rest of the journey.

When I was in New Orleans I met Anja, she became one of my best friends and we remain best friends to this day. Infact in September of the same year I stayed with her in her home in Sweden.

Having already established a friendship with Anja and visiting her in 1986 I returned to Sweden in 1987. I planned to tour Sweden that year and travelled to Stockholm and went on the Viking ship (ferry) to Helsinki. On the ship I met Heidi and Pete from Finland, who I kept in contact with. My experiences there were to be attacked by seagulls and drunks. I was on the tram in Helsinki minding my own business when a drunk sat beside me and then collapsed on me; I pushed him away and jumped over the front seat to escape from him. The seagull was after my buns but I am relieved to say didn't get them.

I also went to Gothenburg and visited a place called Helsingborg I crossed the sea to Denmark at a place called Helsingfors then returned to visit the castle. I was desperate for the toilet and asked someone where I could find one. Someone pointed to a vertical cylinder shaped object and said that's one, it looked like a space aged pod for astronauts. When I approached it I noticed two buttons so I pressed a green one, suddenly it opened and reluctantly I entered. As I got in sure enough there was the toilet so I urinated in the bowl in the conventional way. I then tried finding the flusher, but nothing like that existed not even a button I turned to exit but then thought I would have a last search. To my horror I was consumed by water and my trousers were soaking wet, shocked and surprised I just walked out. It this time when you hope no one has seen you, but as happens to everyone the whole of Helsingborg just happened to be out that day. Thank you for sharing that moment of embarrassment I thought and tried to dry myself off by natural sunlight and the heat from the sunny warm day. Maybe if it had rained no one would have noticed and my dignity would have been in tact, no such luck god 1 me 0.

I took a trip to Canada in 1988 part of the journey was to visit my aunt in Vancouver. However I arrived in Toronto and visited Niagara Falls as well as trek across the provinces of Canada by greyhound bus. The Rocky Mountains were well worth seeing and I even saw a Mounty police wedding. My only mishap there was when I stayed in a hotel in Toronto the fire alarms sounded when I was in bed. Two things occurred I was naked and left the room half asleep had to race back in for clothes and the fact I was at the top of a high building and had at least ten flights of stairs to go down. People were panicking some almost fell down the stairs; it was like an American disaster movie. As it happened it was a small fire in the kitchen near the basement.

My next holiday happened just before I met my ex wife in 1989, I planned a trip to Japan via India. Japan was such an experience venturing from Tokyo to Osaka on the bullet train seeing places on the way and on my return journey. I had written a song about Osaka and was going to see it for the first time. I travelled up the mountains to see mount fugi a large volcano. I found Kyoto a particularly nice place with its shrines and temples, and Nagoya for its busy industrial area. The time went quick there and not until I got back to Tokyo did I experience any funny events. I was in a hostel in Tokyo sharing with three other men, two bunk beds and I stayed in one of the top bunks. It happened first around one o'clock in the morning I heard a click and thud then rustling. God! Rats I thought, then I saw a torch light, then silence. Then at around two the same thing. Again at three, and by four o'clock shouting, swearing and the then I noticed it was a man going in his case. Soon we had all noticed him, one of the other men shouted if you don't pack it in and go to sleep both you and your case are going out that window, and I wont open it either. With that the rest of the night was quiet.

In India I ventured out to Bombay into the streets amidst beggars and prostitutes, seeing many places by taxi as this mode of transport were cheap for me in India. I experienced a cultural shock here with such a class difference from poverty to riches with nothing in between. There was the smell of certain cooking outside that seemed to linger with me on my flight to Japan. When I was at Deli airport I was ask by an armed soldier to go with him in order to identify my baggage. The stairs were slippery, polished marble and so I slipped over and landed at the bottom of the steps. I was tired and bruised and while I was waiting to board the plane was sleeping standing up, leaning against a wall for support.

Although I was in a relationship I did make one last journey alone to Sweden. I wanted to visit Anja and Ulf for the last time. The next time I would see them was in Manchester England for my wedding.

PICKING UP WHERE I HAD LEFT OFF

Sixteen years passed before my next trip abroad I was separated from my wife and free to travel again. Although now I had four children to consider, I had to take into account that they may want to travel with me. I went back to Anja and Ulf in 2007 making that my initial return to travelling. Then I took my younger daughter to Portugal with my mother.

I then went alone to Thailand and met a girl there who I travelled round Thailand with seeing Bangkok and Kon Khan amongst other places the culture seemed similar to India. I visited a snake farm, Temple and other sights as well as Thunya's family. I stayed with her in a beach hut on a private beach listening to wild monkeys at night and watching bright green lizards crawling down the wall.

My boys went on many holidays with me to Sweden, twice to the USA and on a cruise to the Mediterranean visiting

Spain and Italy. I went on an independent trip to Memphis Tennessee, exploring the sights where Elvis Presley lived and died. Followed his journey of life from Tupelo to Memphis. Meeting people that he knew including one of his best friends from school George Klein and a cousin from Tupelo. It was an amazing journey visiting cafes and churches even his father's last home.

The holidays with my children hold treasured memories for me and I have photographs and film footage on my camcorder showing our adventures. I hope they serve as fond memories for them in their future and that they can look back as I do and think of the times we shared. They know I am accident prone and laugh as I fall in slow motion onto the ground after tripping over. Go with style I always say, its part of my life being clumsy I live with it.

I am sure that my children will share holidays with me in the future, my eldest has yet to join me, and maybe we can visit Italy or the U.S.A. I went to San Francisco in May 2012 and carried on to visit Las Vegas and the Grand Canyon. But that venture is for me and this will allow my boys to study at school for a while, then maybe they can join me for further adventures in the future. I must try to avoid accidents and take out holiday insurance; after all I do want to enjoy myself without having the odd accident here and there. Although it does amuse some people and create a few laughs, must avoid dodgy toilets, roofs, slippery floors and the odd moving poles.

San Francisco was quite an adventure mainly due to where I stayed in the city. I took this journey with a friend from work, who proved to be a real character. She is a fun loving person, but when someone or something upsets her she blows her stack. We were staying at the Cova hotel which was right in the middle of a most unsavoury area of San Francisco, people new the area for its soup kitchens, hostels and card board homes. Walking down the street was like entering a zombie movie, bodies walked past in dazed states of existence. No one bothered you unless you looked at them, then they would ask for a dollar, a cigarette or other needy items. At first they seemed quite intimidating but after a while I felt that I could relax around them. My travelling friend felt compassion and began collecting items for them to use, material things like plastic bottles that they could recycle or fruit, bread and other edible items. I said to her "Don't get too friendly or you will find them in your bathroom sleeping in the bath".

My main problem in San Francisco and Las Vegas was getting vertigo trying to cross bridges or walk on high buildings was a nightmare. Los Vegas had a lot of bridges across busy streets I was a nervous wreck at times. The Grand Canyon posed a big problem especially when we had a sand storm, I felt more vulnerable around people, finding it hard to trust them and thinking they would knock me over the edge. Cyclists on the golden gate bridge riding two or three a breast, my head spun and legs turned to jelly. Walking around the top of the stratosphere in Las Vegas feeling as if I was going to fly right out of the window, perhaps I have seen too many American disaster movies.

What I like about seeing places is finding movie locations; San Francisco was not disappointing there. I travelled to Steiner Street to where they filmed part of the movie to Mrs Doubt fire; I was sitting on the steps outside the house imagining the characters standing there. When I got to city hall I imagined Dirty Harry there or at a church where Marylyn Monroe stood outside in her wedding dress. Las Vegas was also the place where movies were made and once one had experienced the bright lights and themed hotels it was time to look at locations.

After all some of the James Bond movies were shot there, not to mention the film 'Hangover' or even the shows over the years like Tom Jones at Caesars palace or Elvis at what was then The international hotel which became the Hilton and now the Las Vegas Hilton (LVH) unfortunately the only memory of Elvis to this day is a statue outside the hotel. No one discusses the fact that he performed there or sells memorabilia.

One of my most memorable experiences from San Francisco had to be Alcatraz (The rock) it was truly amazing and not at all disappointing. Walking around the prison was so eyrie and listening to ex guards and prisoners relating their experience made the place come to life. It is certainly a must for any tourist who wants to experience American history and culture, but don't miss the work shop or the Red Indian protest on the Island. Or the American civil war history of the Island, which people are not so well aware of but plays a major part in the Islands history. Again this place is known for its film locations such as 'The rock' and one of the Dirty Harry movies called 'The enforcer'

When my friend and I visited a car museum I came across a famous singer called Johnny Velvet who made a song popular called 'Blue velvet' He was promoting his book there that included photographs of famous people over the years. He knew Elvis Presley and had a photo taken with Elvis, he also met people such as Johnny Cash, the Beatles and many more. I explained that I had met George Klein who went to school with Elvis and remained one of his friends, Klein became a DJ. At the exhibition was a tribute to Johnny Carson someone else I met years ago who I nearly knocked down some steps in Hollywood. I love travelling because of meeting people and seeing places I like other cultures and ways. We happened upon places which are what I like to do, find a place to have a drink. We did just that in a place in San Francisco, walking up a hill and suddenly finding a small bar that was so lively mainly because of the Elizabeth the bar made/manager, she was amazing drinking and serving drinks. We had pints of beer shots between each drink all very merry and getting merrier. The locals were really friendly and chatty there was no trouble and when it came time to leave ran down the street and hailed a cab or called a taxi. My friend was wrapped round a lamp post and singing once we arrived at the hotel she had a photo taken with the door man and vomited on the flower bed. Once I had got her safely to her room I returned to mine and settled down for the night.

As I have previously mentioned some of the poorer people used to sleep on card board boxes, often seen walking with their card board beds down the street. They went in bins looking for plastic bottles or other sellable items. Some people lie on benches in the day or grass banks around the city, I tried not to stare but at times I could not believe my eyes. I had seen sights in India and Thailand but never in a country like America, My friend Elissa even spotted streakers walking near one of the piers all they were wearing was back packs and smiles.

I was advised to avoid anyone who looked dodgy, but like everywhere I go I seem to attract them, even at home. We were watching a street performance with cars everywhere stylish cars with incredible suspension and hydraulics I was distracted by a man hiding behind branches that he had pulled from trees. Suddenly as someone passed he went boo!!! And popped hi head out from behind the branches, I took a photograph and he shouted "That's a dollar for taking the photo" I took the advice of the locals and continued walking down the street to here him shout "cock sucker, fucking cock sucker"

This was typical of the way the street people were, finding any way to make money. Not far away near the street car (tram) terminal I found a sign which said 'A dollar for weed' at least he was honest about it. At city hall where I jokingly got my friend arrested in order to take a photograph, I was approached again by someone after a dollar (this incidentally increased to five dollars within a few seconds) I offered him a dollar for the paper he had offered me and his reaction as I walked away was "Asshole fucking asshole"

Local people say that these street people are not even from San Francisco and come to the city because people are charitable. They use the money they get for drugs, which they call feeding their habit so we should not encourage them. The Vietnamese are different they search the bins for scraps to sell and feed themselves, Elissa felt compelled to help them as a deserving cause.

My next venture is to New York, I plan to visit ground zero, John Lennon memorial, statue of liberty, central park and other well known attractions. My journey around the world has really only just begun; I have so many sights to see and countries to visit. Gemma is the only one that has never been abroad with me but there is time yet.

I do like local holidays I plan to revisit Goodrington Caravan Park where we used to take the children to their grandparents caravan. I have visited Blackpool many times and worked there. I want to visit Scotland and other places.

CAMPING HOLIDAYS

I have been on camping holidays in England and Wales which was different. Camping is something you either love or hate, living under a canvas for a week or two. Some of us consider this type of holiday as roughing it; this can depend on the facilities and who you go with. Some sites are clean and others not so nice take for instance the camp showers, very basic and sometimes not hygienic with old rusty taps and such. At music festivals people are well catered for as a rule and cant complain about the conditions of the site. Its up to the public to tidy up and be clean of course, in Sweden it is part of their unwritten law of the countryside to keep the place litter free and respect other peoples property.

When I was about nine or ten my father took my brother and I camping. We stayed in a cow field in Dovedale, Derbyshire on a farm. It was fun but I suffered from asthma so had the occasional attacks this disabilitated me a little and I found the walks difficult at times. Despite this I enjoyed visiting the caves and other sites, my brother was always excited to get out and explore and put his foot in cow pat. I lost my telescope down a stream my dad recovered it and was rolling back down his socks when a dog pissed down his leg. I remember eating some (opal fruits) starburst fruity sweets which seemed to help with my asthma for some unknown crazy reason. Perhaps because I had nervous asthma brought on by stress this was relieving my stress.

Later in life during my twenties I went on another camping trip this time with friends and with my own tent that my father gave me it was the same tent we camped in before. I had to put this mountain tent up and tried to follow the instructions, reading them was pointless due to dyslexia, pictured diagrams were easier to follow and made more sense. Despite this I couldn't follow it properly and it was getting dark so my friends helped me, commenting on how long it was taking me and that they got their family tents up quickly. I did say it was a mountain tent and very sturdy, it was used by mountaineers for that reason.

As the darkness fell and rain began to pour on the camp, we all decided to go to bed. During the night the wind began to whistle through the trees and as we were high up in the welsh hills of Monabiar Pembrokeshire it was quite fierce. Suddenly we were in a storm, the whistling wind and following thunder sounded like an air raid as if we were under attack from the air. The next morning I awoke to find all the tents flat and my friends were sleeping in their cars, so whose tent was more stable. Some days were fun, but others monotonous we went for walks and one day went to the cinema.

Today children are used to home comforts and game consoles, so camping to some would be boring and pointless according to your outlook. I should imagine if you have a camper van it might be fun and moving around exploring the area or other places in the country. I enjoyed it but I am an out going person who likes to explore the sights and venture into the unknown. But while I have my health I will continue to go abroad and travel the world, this is because world travel broadens the horizon.

BUILDING LASTING FRIENDSHIPS

*W*hat is building relationships all about; I used to think having a sexual partner and a healthy sex life. Most of my relationships were based on this, no wonder they didn't last. Thinking back yes it was fun, but certainly not a basis for a lasting relationship, after all the sex aspect of most relationships tends to go off after a few years and if that's your foundation what's left. It's like marrying beautiful women you could spend years admiring her looks, but when her beauty fades through old age or whatever else then there is nothing. It's like people trying to retain their youth, futile venture into eventual misery. You can only resurface a road for so long or keep a building up with scaffolding before it eventually collapses. Face lifts, dyed hair and the like then the ultimate falling down of the foundations or seeping through of grey or white hair with a vengeance.

The relationships I had in the past always seemed very odd and not something I could ever base any foundation on, Infact it was like building over a mine shaft or muddy hill. I dated one girl who to be fair made it clear that she did not want a steady relationship, this was made clear when I went back to her apartment hoping for a really good time. We entered her home and I was invited to sit on her settee I took my coat off and relaxed, she announced that she was going to slip into something more comfortable and my imagination went into auto pilot, I visualised a short see through Night dress, nurses uniform or a cat woman suit but knowing my luck it would be a boiler suit or astronaut costume. Open your helmet I want to kiss you or hose me down I am on fire. I heard her shout from the kitchen at the same time I heard a scratching at the door. "Do you like dogs?" she asked. I replied hesitantly "Yes I do"

I expected to see a small dog rushing from the door, judging by the light scratching. Instead of this a big dulux dog came pounding at me like a charging bull and pinned me to the settee. She began licking me, one lick covered my entire face drowning me with her saliva and causing me to choke. When my date reappeared she just laughed and said "believe me you will have better luck with the dog".

Another girl I dated disappeared mysteriously coming home from a club. We had attended her sisters birthday party at her house, we then went for a drink at a nearby pub. On the way back we were both drunk and kissing near a bush, she suddenly fell back and vanished in the bush and I never saw her again. I asked about her but no one ever said where she went.

The strangest experience was where three of us got drunk and slept in the same bed, two girls and myself I slept upside down and had four feet to contend with. Some thing smelt but I don't think it was their feet. My feet were alright because I never had any complaints. I don't remember anything else about that night, but I do know I should never drink vodka because it does the strangest things to me and I can not be responsible for my actions.

I have woken up in many strange places and with odd posters on the wall; I have had really odd relationships and very good relationships. I must confess I have had sex in such funny places too, in the shower, bath and under a Christmas tree to mention a few. Never tried it on a washing machine though, I believe it's a whirl on a spin dryer. I got my toe stuck in the tap in the bath don't know where my other foot went. I suppose experimenting with sex is alright if you take out insurance, by that I mean inflatable dolls can be dangerous. Imagine this being on top of a doll and puncturing it on finding yourself flying out of the window at fifty miles an hour and landing in someone else's pool or a near by tree.

One of my most dangerous experiences was dating a soldier's wife. I thought they had separated and was in a pub with her when she suddenly announced "My husband is coming he is a military policeman and he has brought his friends with him . . . . Hide now!"
Naturally I did as I was told and shot under the table; they all sat down and began to chat while I just lay quietly below them. I heard her trying to encourage them to leave, meanwhile I began to perspire and pray. Eventually the left I don't know how they didn't notice I was there, but I survived.

THAILAND

I really enjoyed my relationship in Thailand but it was short lived as I could not leave my children in England to start a new life in Thailand. I admit I was tempted but my children always come first in my life, this means I can have fun but not get involved in relationships else where. I travelled with a Thai girl around some parts of Thailand, she was a lovely girl and the sex was incredible. We travelled from Bangkok to Khon Khan staying in hotels and a private beach hut; we went to temples and special places to eat. I visited bars and even went on a karaoke night out at her brother's naval base; the family were really kind and polite. It was another life out there.

GATE CRASHING ANNE SUMMERS PARTIES

One of the highlights of my outrageous life was gate crashing parties, this became boring after a while and I needed a new challenge. What about gate crashing Anne Summer parties in drag, acting as a transsexual that would be incredible? I can safely say I have crossed every border and risked life and limb for a laugh, but sitting amongst twenty plus women dressed up and examining sexual power tools. Running round with inflatable willies or kinky undies was a

Was a real laugh, makes one think what are we missing guys? The myth about women inserting vibrators and going on the bus must be true, no wonder they miss their stop, oh no I will have to walk a bit further I here one women comment as she sits back and relaxes for another half hour.

Once the alcohol starts to kick in well, then god knows what will happen, more power tools people losing teeth and need I say more, go for it ladies. More cream and jam on the volevonts and food becomes plentiful sausage rolls with other nibbles, tasty mouth size snacks all round.

PARTIES

I do love parties you get to meet such a lot of nice people, but be warned never be the first there it's so embarrassing. The rules are come about half an hour late, bring a bottle you like or cans, maybe some nibbles in case you don't like their food. In my case stay off the vodka, because I definitely don't remember anything the next day. The stories related back can be pretty bad kissing or snogging girls and saying all sorts of things you regret saying. Then you need to remember where you left your coat and other items of value, because the more drunk you get the worse your memory gets. Importantly find someone interesting to talk to because if it's a bit crowded its hard to pull away from a boring person, once you are drunk it doesn't matter you can listen to crap as well as speak it. Some people are in love with everyone when they are drunk they go kissing every ugly Betty in sight and think they are kissing a beautiful girl or handsome man. Even the ugliest bitch gets a snog, and turn into a frog no one loses out. I like to stay sober enough to see people drop to the ground and make idiots of themselves, slurred speech and in comprehendible words make me laugh.

CHALET PARTIES AT PONTINS

I loved working at Pontins in Blackpool it was an incredible life, the chalet parties we had were well worth attending, it made wife swopping look silly. The chalet keys got thrown onto the table in the middle of the room and you chose one each, I usually got my own key back or a lesbian, not really. The room consisted of lesbian chalet maids, gay kitchen staff, blue coats rarely joined in and bar girls were usually the best dancers etc. The staff were quite poor but the odd bottle of plonk and a spliff or two and the party was underway, well after dealing with the public you needed to unwind. After two seasons things were getting very tiring and the party atmosphere was dying a death. We also competed with each other on who could find a date or get the best girl each week. Sometimes we stole girls off each other and used any means to stop others from getting our girl. The Lesbians played mean tricks to gain control of the situation, by getting up early and going into the food hall first or saying the boss wanted us, or an urgent phone call to distract us. The idea was not to become attached to the guests, but I did and stopped taking part in any more antics, after all I not only fell in love with a guest, I got engaged and later married her.

FROM THE U.S.A WITH LOVE

The all American dream came true in Virginia 1986 when I met a wonderful girl who I considered looked like Diana Ross. She was gorgeous, a true American dream who made my heart pound outside my chest. She had a nice home and a community of good friends that were like brothers and sisters to me. Things couldn't get any better and I had to pinch myself to believe it was really happening, although we were only together for ten days it seemed an eternity. She had so much going for her and I was the luckiest guy alive at the time.

As I have probably stipulated before, people have the habit of copying soaps in their daily life. In fact some people have become so obsessed with soap opera's they stalk actors and sometimes attack them verbally or physically. One actor said because he portrayed an evil mass murderer he was attacked in the street while doing his daily shopping, blue murder in Tesco's or Morrison's maybe yes this is a little extreme but its dangerous acting due to joe public. People follow affairs and then copy them because they think its right because a character from Coronation street or Emmerdale has done it, so it's fine. People watch it religiously and know everything about the characters from year dot or the very first episode. So much so that the new Ten Commandments are out according to the soaps to be followed religiously, this includes;

Thou shalt commit adultery,
Thou shalt steal a bit, but give it back if you get caught.
Thou shalt covert others possessions as long as you give them back,
Thou shall not kill if you can help it
Thou shalt not worship images unless it's a soap star
Thou shalt love your soap star as yourself
Thou shalt not slag your neighbour off, and get caught doing so
Honour your father and your mother then give em hell

Thou shalt not take Norris's name in vein or the rest
says Norris he he
Thou shalt limit affairs to the family or friends, or
anyone within the radius of five miles.
And god helps those who follow that, and that must
be two thirds of the population.

When I think of baths it reminds me of the Barry White
adverts when he popped up from the bubbles of a bath and
said "Its gooooooood". Can't remember what the advert
was for but it took me back to bathroom sex in the bath or
shower which was Goooooood!

HADRIAN'S EYE

I have always been a torment and a prankster; my long
suffering brothers will confirm this. A friend of mine
envied my relationships with girls and once asked me
how I managed to be so intimate with women, I said
its charm and a sense of humour. He once saw me with
an attractive blonde girl and said would I introduce her
to him, I said I would arrange a meeting and as he was
the shy type I would go along to smooth the waters. We
all met at a pub together, Hadrian was nervous and was
asking me questions like how do I get up and close? I
replied be cool and let things happen. When we arrived
the young lady was just arriving I arranged a place to sit
and then ordered the drinks, we started with a general
conversation on horses as Sue had her own horse and
worked at a stable. Hadrian went to the toilet and Sue
asked about my brother, she said he seems nice, this was
my cue to commence with a prank, how wicked am I? I

yes he is but I am biased, however I must say he is very brave considering his affliction. Affliction she looked puzzled, Oh yes perhaps I shouldn't talk about it. Sue was curious so I continued. Yes he has a glass eye and is terribly self conscious, when you look at him he thinks you're looking at that eye, and becomes upset. Also when he leans forward sometimes it falls out.

Hadrian returned and I rapidly changed the subject to holidays and medical insurance. Throughout the conversation Sue kept staring at Hadrian and when he leaned forward Sue rushed forward then sat back.

When Sue went to the toilet Hadrian wanted to know more about her, so I explained about her nervous disposition for example jerking forward not able to keep still, which was of course not true, she was like this because of what I said about Hadrian. He said I know she likes me because she keeps gazing into my eyes, but I was worried about the odd movements like rushing forward when I moved or bent over. On her return Hadrian said he had something in his eye, one of my suggestions to get her to get closer to him, he leaned towards her can you see anything he asked her. She looked at me and then him and asked him does it hurt? He replied no just itchy if I was able to take it out I could maybe find out what it was, then he laughed. She replied don't mind me. He looked very puzzled at this and laughed again.

As the evening drew to a close we walked Sue back home, and then went home ourselves. On the way home he did nothing but talk about Sue and I had to confess about what I had done to both of them. Needless to say my life was hell after that, even with Sue when I confessed to my prank, although we remained friends. I played many pranks after this to so many people; a girl came round my apartment early one morning disturbing me from my sleep so I pranked her.

When she was going down the path almost out of the gate I shouted great night darling same again next week and I will pay extra next time.

I am reminded at this time about my embarrassing moments like getting my penis trapped in the zip of my trousers. I was in Birmingham railway station, listening to the announcements of the trains, suddenly I heard them announce my train and hurriedly finished urinating and tried to put peter away. I let out a yell as I caught the skin of my john Thomas in the zip and was unable to free it. I noticed the blood from all the pulling and was traumatised, the more I pulled the more I bled and it hurt somewhat. Fortunately I was wearing a long coat and just buttoned it up and walked gingerly out to get the train, going down the steps to the platform was agony. I got on the train and sat down trying to get comfortable when I noticed a girl sitting opposite, I had slits in the sides of the coat and got my hands inside them. The train was moving and so rocky it was causing me more discomfort. So I tried again to free Willy I felt a movement and it was free, but not without more pain and blood. The girl must have been watching and observed my sigh of relief; she looked shocked and left at the next stop. Something told me that wasn't her stop, I just hoped she didn't report what she saw and that the ticket inspector didn't want to check my ticket as my hands were covered with blood.

I was happy having relationships and travelling but I always wanted children, I felt it was a missing commodity in my life. Also I often wondered what it was like to get married and settle down, like some of my friends had done. I realised that statistically most marriages ended in divorce but I was willing to try it.

FAMILY UNITY

*F*amily life is fun and can be enjoyable despite some of the down side I was happy in marriage and with my children. I don't think you fully appreciate these time until they have gone, these times are precious and should be lived in the best way possible. Some of the best times in my life have been the Christmas's we shared as well as holidays and other events. I treasure such memories and glad I saved some on camera, video, and DVD.

Memories are the only thing that cant be taken away from you, they serve as happy places to return to in moments of sadness or lonely times. My first experience of Christmas with Gemma my eldest was so wonderful, I had been abroad and bought her a yellow dress, she looked so nice with her strawberry blond hair. That Christmas was one to remember decorating the home and visiting my wife's relatives, we visited mine later. Then when Jennifer was born I had two daughters to share Christmas with, double joy or double trouble. I borrowed a Santa outfit from work and surprised Gemma, she started to cry, which was not the reaction I desired. Christmas was a great time because I was able to watch the children open their presents, they always unwrapped theirs first, before any other member of the family. I have always maintained that no matter who was there, the kids always came first, no one else.

Gemma and Jennifer were in Rainbows at a very early age, this was a club that preceded Brownies and helped them to get involved in many activities. Drawing, painting, written work, and physical activities. They also went on camp once a year which enabled them to socialise with others, away from their parent's supervision. They got involved in nativities and other events such as church parade and carnival events etc.. They entered Brownies after having a ceremony and remained in it until they decided to leave.

My daughters also joined swimming lessons Gemma seemed to get on better than Jennifer, but I think this may have been, because she never got on with the swimming instructor. If Jennie never got on with someone, she would let them know without hesitation. Gemma was more carefree and laid back; she could have a bomb drop around her and not let it bother her. Its so funny how two girls are so different, but I love their individual personalities, they used to object to being dressed the same, but they looked so cute in the same dresses. However I suppose it was like cloning them, I used to look at dresses and visualise them in them, Gemma had strawberry blonde hair, and her sister was a brunette, so the clothes had to suit both of them. Sometimes I would see a nice yellow dress that suited Gemma and a green dress for Jennie, so they did have some styles of their own.

I remember many outings with my girls; we had so many good times that are fond memories for me, such as parks, zoos, shows, cinema, museums and other just as enjoyable venues. Photographs, camcorder films and even tape recordings of their voices, all remind me of their childhood. I used to take the girls to the park in a double pushchair, with food packed in a bag for a picnic. I would take them on the swings and other attractions. It was a nice way to spend the day, just me and my two girls, with no one boss me about, or cause me grief.

I always liked Christmas the best part of the day was opening the presents on the morning, watching the children's faces, full of joy, gratitude for what they received. The preparation weeks before made the day seem worth while, putting the decorations up, and decorating the tree with the children. The only thing that I didn't like was putting batteries in all the toys, why do so many toys have batteries. My children loved playing in the afternoon, the girls had a big kitchen one year that took hours to build, but my girls played so nicely, offering me plastic food etc..

CHRISTMAS WITH THE CHILDREN

Family Christmas had so much meaning for me even as a child myself, the whole atmosphere was magic. Although my parents were hard up they always made it a special event, and one I would remember forever. This is what I wanted for my children, and hopefully I achieved this.

When it came to Christmas time my wife and I would prepare for the event by planning the whole event from the shopping trips to the complete holiday. Things did not always go to plan of course, unforeseen events such as illness or the odd appliance breaking down such as the cooker or washing machine.

We spent time shopping around Manchester in and out of busy shops for clothes and toys, it was hectic but we enjoyed looking and buying, matching clothes, colour coordinating and sometime buying the same items but in different sizes. Once we were home, we prepared the tree (it was bought from a shop around the corner and was our family tree for years) I put the plastic trunk together and opened the branches. The fun was decorating it, we would put on Christmas music and begin trimming the tree, over the years the children would help, adding tinsel, burbles, lights and chocolate decoration, needless to say not all the chocolate ended up on the tree. The tree looked spectacular when it was finished, each year seemed better than the last, and it made a difference when the children got more involved in the event. When the children were at school we hid some of the presents and wrapped them on Christmas Eve, when they were in bed we would sneak down and start wrapping the gifts and put them neatly around the tree. We put them in either sacks or stockings or just in piles with their own names on them, so that they could find their own presents. We would then save one present to put at the foot of their bed, this was in order to occupy them for a while and the tearing of the present would wake us up. Prior to the children going to bed, they would not only leave Santa a drink of alcohol and mince pie, but put a carrot out for the reindeer. Christmas morning was rather special because we could watch the children open their presents, and see the delight on their face, and appreciate what lovely presents they had from both of us and Santa of course (ho ho ho). The children were so involved in the unwrapping of their presents they failed to read the labels and often were unaware they came from. My wife would have black bin liners prepared for the rubbish, so that we would not be buried beneath Christmas wrapping paper, and Christmas music played merrily in the background. Once the event was over my wife prepared dinner and I would construct the toys and put the hundreds of batteries in the items. I once had to put a toy kitchen together, a slide and Thunderbirds Tracy island together. The afternoon consisted of relaxing watching television and joining in family games. Boxing Day was different because all my wife's local relatives used to visit for dinner, and stay for the day, New Year was not as eventful, but the millennium was of course the exception of the rule. I also remember the movies that were always played around Christmas, Jennifer loved the 'wizard of oz' Gemma preferred Ariel 'Little Mermaid' Michael liked sing-along video from Disney and Daniel liked Bob the builder etc..

When the boys were born they offered male companionship to me, this was nice because I was able to do more masculine things. I bought them racing games much like electric racing car games. We played for hours on different games and as they got bigger, we began playing on games consoles; I taught all my children how to use them. I also taught my children board games, how to use the computer and all types of indoor and outdoor sports. I have always wanted the same relationship that my younger brother Hadrian had with his son Adam, not just father and son, but brothers too. The times that we spent together in Blackpool, Manchester, Bury, and Lichfield, going to special places, eating in fast-food places such as Pizza hut, McDonalds and Kentucky fried chicken.

I have so many plans for them, going to venues both in England and abroad my plan is to take them to as many places as I can, and show them as much as I can in the next few years. Childhood memories are precious and should be happy ones, it's important to provide every child with home education, activities and most important your time. The child's future is determined by the way his/her parents are with him/her and how much time they have devoted to them. To shove a child in front of a television or game console and ignore them does nothing for their relationship. Children need exercise, taken to places of interest and educated in many things. Above all allow children to express themselves, teach them good manners and offer love as much as possible. I believe in leading by example, let them learn by the way you do things, show them how to act by what you do and say. A child respects you more if you're firm, consistent and lead by example. My children have grown up with good manners, they don't swear in front of me and they know how to treat others. I have also taught them moral standards, to respect their elders and to help other people less fortunate than themselves. I am pleased to be part of my children's past, although my family life was destroyed by separation and divorce. I do try to keep in as much contact as possible, on the phone, or on the Internet, or whatever means necessary. I bring them on holidays and as many times as I can, between work.

The Swedish trip has to be by far the best, their first flight in a plane to Denmark, followed by a trip on the train over a long bridge to Sweden. They did so much there, having so much fun for the week. The highlight of the trip was the 'Tosselilla' water park and Lund museum. Daniel was a bit funny about his eating, but soon adapted to the environment, in fact he was the one who spoke Swedish first.

Both boys enjoyed being at the airport, and playing Viking games such as 'cubb' the whole experience was really good. But much more was to come, more adventures and an incredible trip to Florida. I have shown my children so much from my past travels now they are joining me on my adventures. Jennifer came with me to Portugal and I am planning to take Gemma to Italy. When I used to sit in the girls bedroom with a globe in my hand spinning it and point to countries at random, I would land on a country imitate the accent and describe the place, food and culture they would sit and listen for hours. My ex wife wondered why I had gone for so long, but the girls enjoyed it so much. Now they can see the places for themselves with or without me. This was one of their fondest memories with me, and I am pleased we shared such times together.

Telling stories was something I enjoyed doing and when my boys were old enough I told them stories too. I believed that you should make the stories come to life, imitate characters and use sound effects, they love these things. A story is only as good as the story teller. Or should be presented like the writer intended it to be. Pictures and sounds, not a droning voice, stimulate children.

Children have vivid imaginations and often conjure up pictures in their minds of characters and events, scenery and progressive movements of characters. Graphic detail is unnecessary for them, but a good story teller can create the scene for them to put their own imagination into practice.

When I took my boys on their ultimate trip to America, they could witness this first hand. Disney world, in Orlando, Florida was a holiday of a lifetime, one in which they could witness something truly spectacular. One mans dream to build a dream place was alive and buzzing with life. If the creator Walt Disney had been alive today he himself would be astonished that his dream had come true. But not only did I take my boys to Disney world, but Universal studios, Kennedy space station and on a boat down the everglades. My delight was seeing them enjoy themselves and sharing their experience. Most fathers would love to do this I am sure, even being with them in the swimming pool and eating out was pleasurable. I filmed each event as it happened for prosperity, knowing that one day they would look back and relive these moments.

In fact my son Michael said that he dreamed about the holiday for weeks afterwards, this made me very happy knowing I had achievement something. Daniel was so impressed with Florida that he said he wanted to live in America when he grew up. I must say they only fought once and argued a little, so that was some achievement for them. They did differ in some of their interests, but I put that down to their individual personalities.

Since living in the midlands away from my children, I have learned many lessons. I miss my children a lot and still get upset when I have to leave them, but I try not to show it. I show them love and affection and yes I spoil them, because I don't see them as often as I would like.

In 2010 I took the boys on a Mediterranean cruise from Palma Majorca to Italy covering Naples and Pompeii they loved it. So much to do on a cruise and the food is marvellous, then in 2011 we returned to Florida covering places we had seen before and others we had never seen. I also went to Memphis in 2010 on a type of Elvis Presley pilgrimage including Tupelo where Elvis was born and meeting George Klein Elvis's best friend from school. At present my boys are studying at school and we advised them that they should put any future holidays abroad on hold until they are older and completed their studies. The holidays with my children hold treasured memories for me and I have photographs and film footage on my camcorder showing our adventures. I hope they serve as fond memories for them in their future and that they can look back as I do and think of the times we shared. They know I am accident prone and laugh as I fall in slow motion onto the ground after tripping over. Go with style I always say, its part of my life being clumsy I live with it.

I am sure that my children will share holidays with me in the future, my eldest has yet to join me, and maybe we can visit Italy or the U.S.A. I do plan a trip to San Francisco in May 2012 and hope to visit Las Vegas and the Grand Canyon. But that venture is for me and this will allow my boys to study at school for a while. Then maybe they can join me for further adventures. I must try to avoid accidents and take out holiday insurance; after all I do want to enjoy myself without having the odd accident here and there. Although it does amuse some people and create a few laughs, must avoid dodgy toilets, roofs, slippery floors and the odd moving poles.

family2002 bw full circle

family a me

ch8

virgina usa 1986 full circle

USA 2011 (41) full circle

mrs doubtfire 2 bw

mike dan pompeii

lynn karen and me bw full circle

jeni in portugal

jeni and ella with owl

grandad 2012 bw

GRAND CANYON BW

gemma and me 3

cruise 2010 1

MIDLIFE CRISES

I must confess when I neared forty I was becoming fearful that I would grow old without achieving everything. How mad is that, when I had achieved so much already by travelling around the world, appearing on radio and television with my own music. Appearing in front of an audience singing and my younger son gave me a buzz and I missed all this so much. When I reached forty I shaved my head and pierced my ears, if someone asked me why I did this I would say I don't know. I was married and my fourth child was on the way, I was diagnosed with dyslexia and trying to understand my condition. I researched into the disability and found that it was like putting a jigsaw together each piece was of the puzzle was an aspect of my life affected by the condition. A collection of symptoms, some of which I would never have associated with dyslexia. I began writing my first book at this time (see my book 'life in a jar-living with dyslexia') I had a tattoo on my shoulder and began to feel trapped in my marriage.

I worked hard in order to build a good home for my family, such as a loft conversion for my eldest daughter. I had the kitchen completely altered into a new one with new units and facilities. I increased the mortgage and had all the windows double glazed. I had new central heating system installed with radiators and a fire place. But this was not enough I wanted more and I eventually went back to university on a mental health course. I met really nice intelligent people who loved travelling and who were planning placements abroad, which made me very jealous and I wanted to go with them. I had to struggle with my own desires of being abroad with such exciting people or living at home in a hum drum existence. I loved my family but felt that the walls were closing in on me and I wanted more and more, such a selfish person I had become.

This is probably typical of someone approaching forty and beyond, and I wish that I knew the answer of how to stop feeling this way. Most people approaching forty have been noted to experience life changes and anxieties that they have struggled to control. Some dye or bleach their hair, have tattoos or body piercing, others drive sports cars or chase young girls or boys. Such extreme behaviour and more could be described as midlife crises and usually occurs from the age of 38 to 45 and can be extremely damaging. Reaching forty is a mile stone in your life and as some say life begins at forty; this should be followed by a government health warning. Life begins at forty and could end at fifty, beware of the drink and bad company. Listening to others can send your life crashing down and leaving you bewildered, although at the time life seems great and going out drinking, dancing and having a ball gives you a real buzz. Like taking something like drugs, being high but suddenly crashing down into depression.

Approaching forty is about taking stock of your life and considering what you have never achieved. It's a milestone in life that is significant because you begin to look at your own mortality, and worry about aging. The odd grey hair appears a wrinkle here or there is a tell tail sign of old age, out comes the hair dye and ant wrinkle cream. The cream fails to work despite the media saying otherwise, it may be simpler to use polyfilla and shave your head, although women may look funny bold. But age affects us all eventually the nicest plum becomes a prune one day, and it must be noted what happens on the outside is going on the inside. The decaying body is telling you to slow down and take it easy, which conflicts with mind that forces you on. You then pay out more and more to rebuild the outer structure and try to put back the moisture into your skin, with loads of cream advertised to re juvenate your body and more products that encourage vitality. In reality you're suspending the inevitable aging process.

On a brighter note, maturity can be an asset, growing up and being more responsible for your actions has got to be beneficial to your children. Rather than falling down drunk or acting so immaturely, this only causes your children to disrespect you. Who wants to think of their parents as drunkards or showing their children up? Parents are suppose to nag you or provide demands on their children, rules that are hard to follow, like control your drinking, don't come in late and don't smoke. For a parent to dress as their daughters or compete with their romantic adventures, is ludicrous, parents just don't act like this do they? Parents are supposed to be parent's not elderly teenagers or Gerry boppers (geriatric swingers), come on parents and act like adults, set an example to your children, help them to understand maturity. I found that hard as I wanted to maintain that stamina and remain physically active in order to continue taking them abroad. But although years of being active and strong enabled me to see places I had to give in and slow down.

But reaching forty is a like reaching a milestone, a mark in your own historical calendar that suggests growing older. Birthday cards help to remind you that the dreaded age of forty has hit you, and it's your last chance to enjoy yourself. The old cliché of life begins at forty triggers a switch in your brain to do something about your life. You look at your children and think, yes why they should have all the fun, it's "me" time. But then what about my appearance, my image. I know I will have a tattoo, dye my hair, slim a little, wear teen fashion, and try to stay young. So what is the formula of eternal youth, the media know, Television commercials suggest creams and potions that apparently work wonders. And in order to feel young I will have a young partner, someone to care for me, provide compliments at the appropriate times. Convince me that I am thirty not forty, and all I need is the stamina of a thirty year old in order to keep up with him/her. But what is really happening, I was reading about a midlife crises, could I be having one of them?

After careful consideration of the facts, I was convinced that Both my wife and I were having a midlife crises at similar times'. Although I don't wish to go on about this it was a contributing factor in my separation. All the signs were there if you know what to look for. Unfortunately people are not well enough informed about it in England until it occurs; they are then faced with the madness and devastation that it ensues. In the United States it is quite widely known, but still considered a myth by some doctors and other members of the multi disciplinary team of professionals. People have mixed ideas worldwide, culture and religion offer other explanations, but in order to put my situation into perspective, I am looking at the midlife crises (MLC) as a factual event.

WHAT IS MIDLIFE CRISES?

This is a question many people ask and usually describe it as a situation that men find themselves in when he or she reach forty. Suddenly he or she go mad and give up a good job, alter their appearance to look younger and chase younger girls. This has been the case for centuries, history has witness many famous people who have experienced this. Kings, Political or religious people of notoriety, those in powerful positions who exploit their subjects. Such people had wives, mistresses and acted in a way to show him or her wanted to be young again.

In today's society particularly in the western world, women seem to taking on this role of going out to work, seeking careers and fighting for equality. Women view family values differently and look at their husband's role as being more than the breadwinner and provider. The male role as father has changed too; fathers are more involved with the bringing up of their children. Thus it is recognised statistically that more women than men are now experiencing the MLC, and for this reason I have written this chapter. I feel by explaining this people can understand why marriages fail, or this can be a contributing factor to most relationships ending so drastically.

It is noted that MLC can start at forty years old, but people have been known to start earlier with some of the initial signs such as anxiety or depression. It is a common feature of middle age thus the term midlife, but it can range from thirty eight to fifty. The condition can last for two years or even eight to ten years. It used to affect more men than women, but this is changing rapidly. The subject can experience emotions such as turmoil, despair, helplessness, distress, dread, disappointment, fear, entrapment in unwelcome restrictive roles. He or she may also suffer from boredom or discontent with previous fulfilling activities or parts of their lives. He or she often question 'Is this all there is?' or feel life has no meaning for them.

The trigger factors are:-

> The realisation of aging/ own mortality physical decline
> Job loss or stalled career
> Unfulfilled dreams
> Questioning your life path
> Marriage trouble or divorce

This is followed by possible outcomes such as sudden changes in personal goals or lifestyle or a life makeover with marriage or career thrown out of the window. Disregarded like an old toy or broken down car, with no regard to the past and its memories.

CHANGES AND REGRESSIVE BEHAVIOUR

The thought that life has been wasted drives some people into wanting to fit in as much activity into their life as possible. With the feeling of having little time left to enjoy themselves and condense a lot of living in such a short space of time, provides them with a sense of urgency. This is evident in their behaviour and sudden drive of energy. It also manifests itself in the way he or she socially interact with others by urging others to copy their lifestyle as if it is new cult or religion.

Some women take on the role of their teenage daughters, by dressing like them and acting as he or she do. This can be embarrassing for the daughters, seeing their forty year old mother dressing so trendy. Watching her displaying herself as an unavoidable catch for men and competing for male attention. Women who are experiencing MLC are like drug addicts who become dependent on a lifestyle, but fail to understand why he or she have no energy to compete with their teenage rivals. One woman described her experience as having an uncontrollable urge to self destruct and wanted to drink herself to oblivion.

There are many experiences of women having MLC and stories told from the prospective of the person who lives with such people. So many sad cases which can be found on the internet, many websites show personal experiences of men and women going through the MLC. Sad because so many marriages are destroyed by this and children suffer as a result of the bizarre actions of the person experiencing MLC.

Regressive behaviour often leads to the person tattooing herself or body piercing. It also results in women going out seeking younger men for excitement, which includes fast cars and night clubs. But age has the habit of catching up with you; you may have the mentality of a teenager, but the body of an older woman. Eventually you slow down, the inner body becomes tired and the outer shell begins to crack. Wrinkles appear and grey roots appear through the red dyed hair, you look at the sagging flesh all over your body and think who am I kidding. I am not so young, or beautiful as my friends once said I was, age has court up with me. My tomboy sees what I do, and his eyes stray to much more desirable women of either his age or younger, and I am left abandoned by him and my children. Alone and abandoned I face the uncertain future with remorse, having just the past to comfort me.

A bleak prospect but very common in these cases, because children have a habit of reminding you of your past. He or she send out bitter messages of how their parents behaved and caused them grief. An example of this is on a chat show called the Jeremy Kyle show, broadcasted throughout the day to a wide audience. This show highlights people's lives by having dysfunctional families as guests sorting out their problems live on the air. Some problems are solved with the help of Jeremy Kyle who faces them with the facts and has no hesitation in telling them exactly what he thinks of their antics. Perhaps he ought to speak to women having a MLC, however I don't think he or she would listen as he or she are running in the fast lane, and unable to stop.

MLC AND ITS PROFOUND EFFECT ON WOMEN

Some women for some unknown reason miss their teenage years, perhaps this is because they are form a broken marriage, their parents could be to blame. However when the women reach forty he or she suddenly get the urge to do what he or she never did, which is sad for them and the family around them. In my ex-wife's case, as I explained previously, she is in a trancelike condition being led by others into a world of make believe, or teen world. Often he or she are led by their new partners, who take over their lives; some even put them in dept, abuse them in countless ways and then leave them to pick up the pieces. Men try to ignore the antics and vice versa should it be happening to men, the idea of that is that their partner will have their MLC and then move on to a normal life again, oblivious to the damage he or she have caused during their MLC.

Some 'weak minded' women put their new partners first before their children, still expect them to respect and love them. In my opinion he or she are not fit to have children and should live single lives, so many mothers seem to adopt this carefree attitude, which was once considered a male trait.

The society has changed and given women a new lease of life, once considered an unfitting was to act, married women used to stay at home and care for the children. The men used to go out to work and earn the money, go home to a cooked meal, pipe and slippers. The man would tend to the garden and be classed as head of the household, his word was final and the woman knew her place in life. Now some women believe in the modern husband who fits their needs, he or she use sex as a reward for good deeds, he or she appear to love them, but are out for selfish gain. Some women are more concerned with social activities than their own home, he or she dress to impress and lead men into their home, offering them all manner of things.

MLC seems to enhance this situation, driving women into (sometimes) unknown territory, giving them a sense of ecstasy not encountered before. He or she become flattered by the attraction of younger men/women, deluded by their own youthful looks, which is only seen by them in the mirror. He or she hear what he or she want to hear and disregard the rest, anything complimentary that elevates them to new heights. However all he or she see is not real, only what appears to be real, just like their artificial existence brought about by their MLC, it is described as a fast exciting life, which is often followed by disaster.

The only way out of a MLC is for the person to come out of it on their own, no one can help them because the person won't listen to anyone. Like depression, the person has to come to a realisation that he or she require help, and then seek it from whatever source necessary, whether it is from the GP, counsellor or other profession. Sometimes friends can offer support; depending on the type of friend and their state of mind some can make matters worse. To acknowledge that he or she are experiencing an MLC is a start, admitting to themselves that a problem exists helps them to come to a realisation that he or she have destroyed they're home and the relationship with their children, by selfishly seeking their own desires. Living with someone with MLC is like living with a time bomb, you don't know when he or she are going to go off.

However without dwelling too much on this subject I must confess by being amused at peoples antics while travelling through this stage in their life. All is it out of their control it has an element of irony as he or she attempt to pursue a youthful existence by using cosmetics and clothes from places such as new look and other youthful stores. Most MLC victims are seen amongst teenagers trying to fit in by dressing like them and putting on layers of make up, often using bad techniques and looking like divas rather than glamorous ladies. By this I am in no means criticising anyone and do not want to offend any one by my remarks, but I do think this experience was factual and one of the causes of my separation.

The rest was down to me and my feeling trapped and unable to pursue my ventures successfully while I was married, travelling abroad again has given me new wings and allowed me to experience life once more perhaps that's my MLC who knows. I don't blame my ex wife totally for my separation and consider her a good mother who cares about her children, she is the stability in the family unit and the children are close to her which is excellent. I am reassured that if the children are poorly or who have problems she deals with it sensibly. I do wish communication with us was better so that we could discuss the children more often, but I realise that her partner would probably not approve of our friendship. So I am content with third hand information and the odd story filtering through regarding the children's progress.

SURVIVING SEPERATION

*M*y way of surviving separation was to imagine my partner had died and so I began a grieving process denial came first the aspect of not excepting it had actually happened then anger which lasted quite a while and the area of acceptance only came about when I wrote my second book 'Rise of the phoenix—a fathers story' when I vented my feelings about the separation and described the entire event from the separation, divorce and my leaving Manchester.

The main problem was moving into a private rented flat and trying to survive; I was also working and having so many problems.

I moved again this time in a private rented house that became known as the house from hell. The house from hell involved a leak in the bedroom I invested in a bucket to catch the drips and an umbrella in case the leak got worse. I also had a hole in the bathroom and bricks that had fallen from the loft into the bath, luckily my children were not in the bath at that time. It was a draughty house, cold and my eldest daughter thought it was creepy. Outside the house was noisy and often road works made things even more difficult. My younger daughter was living with me at the time and actually had an accident outside the house due to road works. She nearly fell down a hole.

After leaving the house of hell, and my adorable children. I travelled south to the midlands, to a place I grew up called Lichfield in Staffordshire. I found it hard to leave my children in Manchester, there were tears and sadness, telling them that I had to leave was the hardest thing that I have ever done. I explained the circumstances why I had to do this, having no job and a large rent to pay made it difficult to survive. In reality I was homeless, jobless and depressed. Although I knew my younger children (my boys) would probably not understand, my older children (my daughters) would, and could explain to the boys.

The purpose of this book was partly to explain to them about my life and about how I reached normality. I liked family life and particularly enjoyed taking my children out to places that they had never been, new experiences and adventures. After all that is the purpose of my life to explore and enjoy new things and it is a bonus with my children. Separation is never easy and is often painful; no one wants to separate especially after sixteen years. The years of getting to know each other and working together as a family, to create a life together with the thought of being together forever as you planned at your wedding. Suddenly that's all gone as is the family home that was altered and worked on to accommodate your family.

Years of building, destroyed in seconds after separation, never to be seen again, only the memories remain nothing else. My way of coming to terms with this was to pretend that my wife had died and that I was the grieving widow this came surprisingly easy to me I must admit. Maybe I was really grieving after all I had lost her, the person I once knew did not exist any more and I was left with a person I didn't know, a stranger. And with this thought in mind I moved on. Surviving separation however meant more than erasing her memory from my mind, We had children together and they had to be considered, people forget that separation often means the father has to not only leave his wife but the children as well. Often the hardest part is leaving your children behind and not seeing them every day. I used to play a DVD movie called Mrs Doubt fire over and over again because it reminded me of my circumstances, dealing with a fathers life after separation. The law favours the women/ mother not the man, often men have no say when it comes to bringing up children, excluded from so many things like parents evening at school. Robin Williams's portrayal of a separated dad so desperate to see his children he dressed as a woman and applied for a job as house keeper/child minder at his children's home. Successful for a while he saw his children regularly until something went wrong and so the story continues, but the point I am making is that although we want to see our children it is sometimes not possible and we often feel left out and made to feel like an outsider while our ex partner introduces a new man into their lives.

Through circumstances we see less and less of them and it hurts, but you keep going building your own life. You try to compensate by taking them on special holidays, giving them gifts and inviting them to stay with you for weeks a time, but nothing ever makes up for the time they share with their mother. So those are considered lost times and irreplaceable gaps in your life. No one will ever understand the times when you think of your children during those moments of loneliness and thinking I wish I was with you right now. The times you miss are when they come home from school with their work and show pictures to you or share their achievements or awards, proud young faces awaiting praise from you or teatimes when you eat together or go to the movies.

CHANGING COURSE

*H*aving reached the turning point in my life I began to make plans for my future. This was when I had moved to the midlands and found work again; life was beginning to look up at last. A new beginning was in order in a place where I grew up, meeting old friends and catching up with their lives. Almost twenty years had passed since I had seen these friends and they had pursued careers and had families of their own. I had returned to care work with a positive attitude and as a qualified nurse given full support and further training, uninterrupted my activities in Manchester.

I was out at parties, my social life had improved and I had continued to meet old friends and new ones. One recent event was at work where the Dignity awareness project was introduced by senior nurse Amanda Davies who motivated all of us to educate all staff into putting such activity into practice. Another friend and colleague Stephanie Sanders created a poem for the occasion which reads as follows;-

Dignity awareness

Can we swap for an hour or two?
You be me and I'll be you
Someone's daughter, someone's son
Busy with life getting things done
Doing the things I want to do
Dependant on no one, not having a clue
What was in store in the future for me?
That the person I was, could anyone see?
Remember please that I was so young too
I held down a job, could have looked after you!
Live life to the full, that's what I say
I haven't always been this way
So as I sit in my chair or lie in my bed
Think of the life I may once led
Remember these words as you care for me
Please treat me with kindness and dignity

S Sanders 20/1/2012

I was inspired and encouraged by many people, but my colleague and friend Amanda Davies RGN was a true tower of strength in this project explaining how she was going to handle Dignity and educate some of the staff. Of course other staff also encouraged me and helped to build up my confidence again. I was working in the general and mental health nurse settings and felt I was completely renewed as a person. So many staff encouraged me to work hard and enjoy my work again. Socially I had also began to enjoy myself out at parties including shed parties as I called them (private bars in garden sheds) joined by staff from work. My injuries were a demonstration that I was having fun; I would get drunk and fall over or throw up over someone's prize flowers. I had a large bruise from my behind right down the back of my leg through falling and hitting my leg on a toilet. I have bumped my head many times too and live to tell the tale. Its funny how life goes by and when you look back you realise that you did so much. Its only when you come to reflect on things that you say to yourself 'god did I do all that or how did I do so much in so many years, or why am I talking to myself'. It begs the question what am I going to do next?

LIFE GOES ROUND IN CIRCLES

I think it's true that life goes round in circles, we tend to go about our daily business and something always reminds us of the past.

A place maybe or an event in the day perhaps some kind of music or lyrics in a song, an aroma of perfume or tobacco, a television program or photographs.

Strangely enough Amanda Davies showed me a photograph taken at Lichfield bower years ago with a monkey; I found a photo of my brothers and I taken in the same place, the same year with possibly the same monkey.

I have crossed paths a number of times with people, another colleague and friend Carol Aston I worked with years ago and as children we lived in the same neighbourhood, knew the same people and never met until we worked together at Nearfield house. Just one example of how our life tends to run in strange patterns something to think about when your sitting alone in a café watching people passing by or travelling on public transport trying to avoid the nutters who insist on sitting next to you, because you have a friendly face and seem to listen to their mad chants. Its time to look out of the window and reminisce about family, friends and places you love most of all.

Going full circle is about just these experiences of reuniting friends and sometimes picking up the pieces left behind. I am reminded by friends about the past and music brings back so many memories of school life, early teens, married life and travel. All around the world visiting places certainly inspired me to write this book, this along with seeing my childhood home and going full circle.

WHY RELIVE THE PAST

*I*t is good to reflect on the good times, but not dwell on past events. Or indeed get stuck in the past thinking about what could have been, often things can get depressing when this occurs. Oscar Wilde once said "One charm of the past is that it is the past". While Golda Meir stated that "One cannot and must not erase the past, merely because it does not fit the present". Two conflicting quotes but equally as meaningful and thought provoking. However the next quote seems more sensible because it refers to the here and now. "With the past, I have nothing to do nor with the future. I live now". Ralph Emerson. I believe we learn from our past and that we have good memories to reflect on when bad times are present. So "What you need to know about the past is that no matter what has happened, it has all worked together to bring you to this very moment. And this is the moment you can choose to make everything new, right now". Unknown author. One person responded to a question why do people feel the need to dig up the past saying "cause graveyards are full of treasures" another response was "depends whether or not there are skeletons in that closet".

Bad memories can return in moments of stress or trauma, smells, visual things like objects or items of clothing, perhaps a movie can spark a memory that was pushed at the back of your mind. It is important therefore to address past issues, visit a counsellor or someone that can help you discuss past issues. Only when you have addressed past events or traumas can you successfully move on.

Memories can be nice and in your twilight years these can serve as a comfort to you. The aspect of living in the now is to build memories for your future, by being adventurous and fulfilling childhood dreams. Some dreams may not reachable such as climbing Mount Everest, swimming the Pacific Ocean or being an astronaut. But to travel to China or Canada can be fulfilled by making the effort to plan the journey, book it at a travel agent and work for the money to get there. Some people have had tragic times as a child in which case reflecting on the past would be too upsetting to contemplate, living in the present has to be the only answer, to build a life on present events. People often look at the past in order to learn by past mistakes, politicians look at historical events to organise a structured society. General and other senior officers look at historical battles formulating strategies to conquer enemies, famous battles that have been won only by drawing on past strategies to achieve victory. But in every day society we look at people living together in a peaceful community and team spirit. During the Second World War it is said that everyone pulled together to help survive the blitz and other unpleasant events of the time. Society as a whole was based on everybody helping each other and neighbourliness that has never been seen before or again since this time. Does it take a disaster to cause such unity amongst people, because judging by society today it's a matter of going to work, coming home and shutting the world out?

Some blame the invention of such things as game consoles, television and other equipment for the lack of community spirit. But had we been at war today would we get the same thing as before. Does it take the dropping of a few bombs here or there to get people to communicate with their neighbours? Don't get any ideas about that I would like to lose my accommodation just to speak to Mrs Smith or Mr Brown. And I hate the idea of someone just coming into your house via the back door and using it as an open house. Putting on your kettle, critising your curtains or noisy clock and trying to advice you on how to live your life or bring up your children. I used to hate some people doing that with my parents and then when I was first at my ex wife's house this was like an open house with access for family and neighbours, often people used to walk in and appear in the living room. I was once painting a ceiling when a man appeared I was taken by surprise until he announced that he was my girl friend at the times uncle. Not being used to this and the fact that it was her grandmother's family home I was a little bewildered by the open house policy. One moment you're alone the next invaded by friends and neighbours of all description.

Relatives also expect the house to remain the same, but time does not stand still changes take place and you can't expect a place to remain either as a shrine or museum in order to preserve memories of lost ones or a forgotten childhood. Part of living in the past involves these things and by doing this one tends to lack the reason for progression and moving on to new life. Often it is useful to film family events and keep family videos or DVDs; these can be viewed by future generations or by parents who are looking back at family life years into the future. I consider this as being healthy mentally, but to keep a room with all the persons belongings around as if they are still alive, maybe that's disturbing. I am not saying don't mourn for them and keep the odd memory of them, but an entire room dedicated to them or a complete shrine may be a little much.

Having said this I did venture to Graceland and see places that Elvis Presley lived in, rooms and the gardens of his home in Graceland, where all his rooms remained in tact which included a jungle room, dining room, lounge, TV room and pool room but other places where he had suits, jump suits from concerts and gold records displayed on the walls. It seemed quite eyrie in the jungle room like Elvis was still present there, I later found out that he spent a lot of time there and that it was his favourite room.

The problem is when you get stuck in the past unable to move on due to past events or traumas. People such as rape victims who are reminded of their trauma by smells, visual sights like someone looking like the predator or predators. Reliving the events in nightmares or by seeing events on television. One of the worst things is not being believed or blaming yourself for putting yourself in that position, if it hadn't have been for me doing this or that it wouldn't have happened, but in reality it shouldn't have happened anyway. Why should the victim feel guilty and not the one who conducted the act, who has the right to abuse anyone else in this way. This has to be one of the worst acts of abuse and punishable by castration or something equally as affective. Society is too soft on rapists and child abusers and the victims suffer worse than they do. Perhaps they should have national castration day were all abusers stand in a stock and have their bits cut off with a pair of shears. Donkey dick day or all ball day all the big nobs invited just a thought.

LOOKING AHEAD

I think it's true that we make our memories on a daily basis, by doing something maybe achieving something. Our holidays each year or even day trips become memories to us we take photographs or film events and look back on them as fond memories. But we then plan more holidays and move forward to experience further events to reflect on. My mind is always active which is why I write such a lot, I tend to plan ahead with holidays and events, but am spontaneous when it comes to daily activities. I can just get up and think I will go out here or there at random, or just jump on a bus and travel somewhere different. I don't like planned holidays where everyday is organised in advance, this tends to mess with my head. I believe in being relaxed and let the days events take place without fuss or endurance. A too structured day reminds me of work and when you're on holiday you don't want to think of work.

Having said this how many times have you been on holiday and someone asks you 'what do you do for a living?' The dreaded question that you know will lead to someone telling you about their ailments or going on about their operation. Imagine eight hours on a plane listening to someone's hernia operation or showing you their rash. What's this lump on my leg or breast someone asks as you are eating the horrid in-flight meal, revealing a pussy wound as you guzzle your soup. I even had to take some elderly man to the toilet at one hotel for a family and so I don't let on that I am a nurse instead I am a brain surgeon or psychiatrist. Try and tell me your tale now and I will have you certified; leave me to watch the in-flight movie about a flight that crashed like 'Airport' or snakes on the plane.

The link between work and social life should be separated allowing you to be free from thinking about work. However in my occupation it is difficult as we come across so many situations that require our help, such as accidents or trauma's. so the need for us to act in any given situation is vital for helping people. We have a duty of care not just at work but in the community even when we are on holiday. We can't ignore someone in distress and we should offer our serves if required, these are the benefits of being a nurse. When I was in my family home in Manchester I used to always have people knocking at the door to help children or adults who were injured in some way.

One day I was preparing a salad in the kitchen when I witnessed an accident. A cyclist got knocked down by a lorry and was thrown off her bike. The bike was mangled under the front wheels and the cyclist was lying on the grass bank. I dropped my knife and ran out of the front door towards the cyclist who by then had jumped to her feet and was cursing the driver. She was clearly not hurt but more concerned about her bike.

I have dealt with collapsed old ladies in the street, a man fell down stairs on a bus. I revived someone in the swimming baths who had been fitting and I could tell you many more stories. What I wouldn't like to do was give mouth to mouth to a tramp or drug addict not a pleasant thought or one I would ever like to encounter. I hope another nurse or first aider is present for that pleasantry, good luck with that one. A case of share my second hand booze or dinner from earlier.

THOSE WHO INFLUENCED MY LIFE

Many people have influenced my life my childhood was influenced by action heroes as I was a peony child, skinny and crap at fighting, Superman was my favourite hero I imagined being strong and able to fly out of danger. As I grew so did my ego and I became more confident and able to conquer the world without a cape. I then looked at more rebellious roles trying to seek my own identity as a teenager at this time such people as James Dean influenced me in his portrayal as a rebel in the movie 'Rebel without a cause' and Elvis Presley's character in such films as 'Wild in the country' and 'Roustabout' I used to play protest songs such as John Lennon's 'Give peace a change' and 'Working class hero' played them loud and sang along to them. My parent shouted turn the music down and they hated some of the lyrics because of the swearing and anti social innuendos.

As my life changed so did my taste in music, but I never forgot the songs that inspired me from one generation to the next. Through the generations song writers have written about life, places and about love and some songs will never die. They become classics like George Harrison's 'Something' and 'Here comes the sun', John Lennon's 'Imagine' Simon and Garfunkel 'Bridge over troubled water' Paul McCartney 'Band on the run' The Beatles 'All you need is love' and many more. Neil Diamond wrote songs for The Monkee's like 'I'm a believer' as well as singing many of his own songs 'Love on the rocks' being a personal favourite. But the eighties and nineties brought about some amazing artists too my daughters used to like Take that, The spice girls and many more. My boys like Paramore who are presently popular so the years go on and my grandchildren are listening and watching artists like Jessie Jay, Cheryl Lloyd and such. I wonder what they will think back on as they here music from their past.

REACHING FULL CIRCLE

ulfilment is achieved by being satisfied with life and in reaching full circle, meeting teachers from my school caused me to reach full circle, as I showed them the progress that I had made academically, attending university for almost five years and gaining two diploma's to my credit. Showing that with my own merit I could be successful, being self taught and tolerating years of rejection, bullying and criticism. I came out laughing and proving that a dyslexic person can succeed; obviously I am not the first and won't be the last. Many famous people are dyslexic as are everyday people like myself, Sir Winston Churchill, Albert Einstein, Tom Cruise, Cher, Jackie Stewart and the list goes on.

As I have previously mentioned, I am fascinated by peoples live and how some reach success in rags to riches stories J.K Rowling is one such person who came from a humble back ground to create the character who we know today as Harry Potter. She was inspired her surroundings in Chepstow and Deans forest among other places. She wrote her first novel as an unemployed single mother and rose to success to become a millionaire with Harry Potter a household name all over the world.

One thing I do believe is you never forget your roots, my parents were a good support to me, they were strong personalities and maintained a stable relationship until my father's death. I like examining the lives of the rich and famous, not the one who were born rich but those who struggled from poverty to riches or as some would say rags to riches. Elvis Presley, John Lennon and many more really inspire me. Elvis was one who I studied as he came from a humble background to become a rock and roll singer, influenced by gospel and country music and forming his own style of performance that we know today. John Lennon who was also inspired by rock music and Elvis's performance created his own sound with the Beatles showing that the boys from Liverpool could be successful by their own efforts. Naturally we all need someone to give us that extra shove; Elvis had many people who supported him. The Beatles had Brian Epstein amongst others, the list of success stories is endless, and this demonstrates positive attitudes and those who believe in you and what you can achieve. They say behind every great man is a woman and I believe that to be true. I was supported by my ex wife of that I have no doubt, I didn't recognise that at the time, but looking back this was the case. Reaching full circle can occur at any time in your life, because it's all about revisiting aspects of your past and enjoying fond memories.

TWILIGHT DAZE

Sometimes in peoples twilight years they think back and recaptured the best aspects of their lives. Faded memories of their youth with friends or relatives who shared their lives at that time, Seventy or eighty years of life relived in moments some are fortunate enough to write about these events and others peoples experiences die with them. I am fascinated by people's lives often by pop stars and actors lives as they struggle to become famous. The Beatles are such an example as they all came from Liverpool and started from a working class environment to reach fame and fortune. Often those who struggle and become successful appreciate their roots and value their achievements; they often revisit their past and go full circle by appreciating where they came from and the people who influenced them. Twilight daze is an idea for a new book I thought about writing a book about a nursing or residential home based on my experience. I have many characters from my working life to use in this story and the setting based on one home from my past, calling the place 'Twilight daze'. I would make it a light hearted comedy reflecting on the amusing aspects of caring for the elderly, an area that most people would relate to and find funny.

SELF ANALYSIS

The philosophy of life is one of consistently examining your life and exploring the reasons for doing what you do and justifying your actions.

The significance of reaching full circle is about discovering your true self and summarising your past. Its all about taking stock of what you have done and being satisfied with your achievements after all at the end of the day its only you who have to live with that. No one else can say to you what you have done and that you should never have done something. You and your conscience have to decide whether or not you have done wrong and live with it. And the achievements that you make are for your own gratification, although others may share your success and be proud of you.

When life goes full circle, its like seeing your self in a mirror the reflection is a visual display of your life, every wrinkle, every expression tells a different story, a scar exposes an unfortunate trauma in your life. When I look in the mirror I see my father looking back at me, I see him in me and suddenly he is there to advise me and help me along. I see my mother although she's alive, supporting my father with a gentle prod to encourage me to act wisely and cautiously. But full circle is also about meeting past friends and relatives who influenced me in my early stages of life, like my aunty Penny and Dorothea. People who had and have inner strength to guide me and influence my life, by sharing knowledge and caring about my feelings. To this degree full circle happens for me, reflecting on events and not revisiting the past, at least not being locked into the past. I take the healthy option of seeking comfort from past events and using past experiences to plan my future.

I remember such happy times in my childhood, my teens though turbulent were also happy. I think of my twenties as a transformation from teenage trials and tribulations to reaching maturity. Then my travel days from twenties into my thirties, until my married and family life from thirty to fifty. Again my travelling from forties to fifties and need I go on. You have shared some of my highlights and low lights in this book; I hope that I have demonstrated how people go full circle and that you make your own life and create your own future. I may have made many mistakes in my life, but I have enjoyed being married and travelling the world. My legacy lies with my children; they will judge me as they wish and remember me as a Father first and then a traveller. They will always be with me in my heart no matter where I am or what I do, I will always love them. And when they reach full circle I hope they will remember the good times we shared together as a family and afterwards. Both my children and grandchildren remember I love you all very much.

I was looking in facebook talking to my children when I decided to search for the Sutherlands, a family I had grown up with. My mother said she wanted to contact her friend Eileen years ago but despite effort I could not find them. Finally I found Karen despite being older she seemed the same such as the same cheeky grin. She put me onto Jennifer and I felt again that I had reached full circle, for the girl I had grown up with was speaking to me on the phone. Strange that my brother and I used to compete for her attention and that so much time had gone by.

Another person I met from the past was Sue Copeman (now called Giess) we had been to a concert together as well as performed in a amateur singing group. We sang round pubs for children in need and they also sang backing vocals on one of my songs called 'Modern Egypt'. Sue came with me to see Paul McCartney perform at the Birmingham National exhibition centre (N.E.C) What a performance, I went back to see him again but forgot about the explosions during the song 'Live and let die' and I was situated right next to one of them. I jumped off my seat and nearly had a heart attack.

Seeing Sue reminded me of those days but this time we were more intimate and she too had four children which was nice for us. We discussed our past together and what had occurred between us meeting again, so much had happened in our lives. We went to restaurants and other places, she came to my flat and I visited her house. I introduced her to my boys when they stayed with me in order for them to get to know her. Things went well and the years that had passed between our last meeting didn't seem so long although by my calculations it was over twenty years. This made me think again that I had met my past once more, I had reached full circle.

Meeting Mick Morris and Brian Marshal made me look back on my school years and I revisited Netherstowe school as I did Chadsmead school. Walking the corridors, as I did as a child and teenager. Remembering past events in the classrooms and assembly hall, although some changes had taken place it was still recognisable and the longer I was there the more the memories came back.

Mick Morris had assisted me with moving from Manchester to my childhood town of Lichfield, he also helped me to readjust after my ordeal in the house from hell in Manchester. I felt like the phoenix rising from the ashes to be reborn into a new life, a lot of people were very supportive and for that I am very grateful. One of my work colleagues Joy Sage helped me greatly to build up my confidence at work she amongst many others gave me my confidence back and my spark of life had returned.

When I was still in my marital home in Ashton U Lyne (Manchester) Mick Morris had contact me on the internet via friends reunited. It was such a surprise to hear from him and he was then invited up to visit the family. He informed me that that a school friend was living just around the corner in Dukenfield and he arranged for us to meet in a pub in Dukenfield. Although we met Brian was acquainted with my older brother who at that time was a policeman and he never liked for whatever reason and miss trusted me. I was never really close to Brian as I used to be closer to others such as Gordon Nash who I see now and then.

Mick remains a friend who being a snooker player invited me to the clubs to watch him play in tournament. Mick has won trophies and met celebrity snooker players, he even played Hurricane Higgins a professional snooker player. Mick had reached his ambition in snooker by winning such trophies and had fond memories of past events like achieving high breaks in the sport.

Mick has a really nice close family unit which I envy very much. I miss not having the family around me and having a close relationship like he has with his wife Lynette. True is the saying you don't know what you've lost until its gone. Sixteen years being together was a long time and you tend to do the same things when you split up like buy the same furniture and even buy the same groceries. I once phoned my ex wife while I was shopping to make sure I was buying the right products for my boys in a way she had gone shopping with me. Perhaps the fact we had produced children together a little bit of both of us were instilled in our children and we see their characteristics in them. Also the grandchildren Ella and Oliver bring a certain family unity back together in order to show them normality and the peace we once had has been restored. All the anger and bitterness put aside so that we can all be happy in our own family environments because many family event are yet to come such as weddings, christenings and birthday parties.

I know looking back when I return home to Manchester I will remember all my friends and colleagues here and think of happy events such as shed parties (peoples private bars) staff outings, weddings and other occasions. I will laugh out loud at the clumsy accidents that I have had such as slipping in the toilet and bruising my leg. I will remember the fact vodka doesn't suit me and the situations that I found myself in due to that, as well as the rumours after the event. Yes as I take stock of my life I have had some fun times which definitely out weigh the bad times, I can certainly say I have enjoyed life.

And so I say in order to reach full circle it is important to keep a grip on past events, treasure your memories and maintain contact with your family and friends from the past. That is to say not become obsessed with the past, but maintain contact so that you don't regret anything. Even if you contact them a few times a year, you are aware they are well and happy. Don't be afraid to visit old places that you once lived but don't expect them to stay the same, just think I was there once and did have some good times there. At this point you will reach your full circle.

PEOPLE WHO HAVE INSPIRED ME AND INFLUENCED MY LIFE

My parents Rita Sutton and Leonard Sutton	Role models
Aunty Penny	My mentor from my childhood to present
Gran and Grandad Sutton	guiding lights
Nan and Granddad Perruzza	Guidance
My children Gemma, Jennifer, Michael and Daniel	Being there for me and sharing their love

Aunty Mary who I shared some of my life with and so many memories

Friends Carol Aston, Richard Howarth, Anja and Ulf, Mick Morris, Anne Donagon, Joy Sage, Angie Nicholls, Julie Smith and many more

John Lennon	Music and lyrics life style
Paul McCartney	Music and supporting charity
George Harrison	Music lyrics and charity
Elvis Presley	songs performances life story
Simon and Garfunkel	music and lyrics

Neil Diamond and many more celebrities

To all my friends and colleagues bless you all xxxxx

WHAT IS LOVE

*L*ove is not measured by words but by deed, action speaks louder than word, however it is nicer to hear the words expressed. I love you, comes affectionately from a child's lips in all sincerity as the child speaks from honesty and straight from the heart. It's the type of love that cannot be measured and unconditionally is given with a smiling face or embracing arms. Act of kindness done through devotion from those close to you and without reward just that of love. I will do it for you, because of you and all for you. I commit myself to help and cherish you all because I love you.

THOSE IN GRIEF

Wipe a tear, from a mourning eye,
and please remember, I wanted to die,
my life seemed to last so many years,
so don't cry, don't shed your tears.

Open your eyes, raise your head,
it's not your fault, that I am dead,
I loved you dearly, with my heart,
so be not sad, now we're apart.

I drank to you, my last farewell,
and left fresh flowers for you to smell,
I left a rose, pressed in a book,
near a verse, please take a look.

I'm happy now, I rest in peace,
my painful body, had to cease,
now at last I'm free from pain,
you are able to live again.

MY FRIEND THE BOTTLE

Drink a glass of wine with me
Drink it down instead of tea
Drink a toast to new lost friends
Have another till the bottle ends.

My friend the bottle is always by my side
My friend the bottle knows when to hide
My friend the bottle is close to hand
My friend the bottle is always in demand.

So drink to my health
Drink to my wealth
Drink to the birth of a child
Drink until you're reckless and wild.

Drink to a new life to begin
Drink whisky or even neat gin
Drink lager or drink beer
Not just parties, but all year.

But then stop!
Be in control
Don't lose your character
Or public role
Think of others
Who may get hurt
Why roll in the gutter
Or in the dirt?
Are you that desperate
To sink that low
Or have you no will-power
To just say no?

FACING DESTINY

I feel at peace,
Within my soul,
Now at last my mind is whole,
For life's great pleasures are no longer mine,
I no longer feel my body entwined,
By problems of how I must be fed,
Or how long I will sleep alone in my bed,
I foresaw my destiny deep within my mind,
I felt myself in ecstasy examining my find,
So now I look up to you with my mind clear and bright,
I am up above I'm looking at you through the star above,
I say to you,
Who I once knew,
Do you believe it so?
For let me tell you now it's time for you to go.

Printed in the United States
by Baker & Taylor Publisher Services